NATURAL HAZARDS AND DISASTER MANAGEMENT

NATURAL HAZARDS AND DISASTER MANAGEMENT

Editor

Dr. B. C. Jat

Lecturer in Geography

Government P. G. College

NEEM KA THANA, RAJASTHAN

MD PUBLICATIONS PVT LTD

New Delhi

Published by

MD Publications Pvt Ltd
"MD House", 11, Darya Ganj, New Delhi-110002
Tel. : +91-11-41562846, 41563325
E-mail : contact@mdppl.com
Website : www.mdppl.com

ISBN : 978-81-7533-126-6

Price : Rs. 795.00

Printed and Published by **MD Publications Pvt Ltd** at Times Press, New Delhi

CONENTS

Pages

Preface

1. ENVIRONMENTAL HAZARDS AND DISASTER: MEANING AND CONCEPT
—*Dr.D.K. Thakur* 1—62

2. VULNERABILITY ANALYSIS AND MITIGATION-KEY TO DISASTER MANAGEMENT
—*R. B. Singh* 63—69

3. NATURAL HAZARDS AND DISASTERS: MANAGEMENT FOR SUSTAINABLE DEVELOPMENT
—*Prof. B.L. Teli* 71—76

4. ROLE OF REMOTE SENSING AND GIS TECHNOLOGY
—*Rajesh Kumar and Girdhari Lal Yadav* 77—85

5. MAJOR INDIAN EARTHQUAKES (AFTER 1956) & ITS IMPACT ON INDIAN ECONOMY
—*Ravindra Pratap Singh* 87—99

6. DEVELOPING AN ASIAN TSUNAMI WARNING SYSTEM
—*Naresh Kumar Verma* 101—107

7. DISASTER MANAGEMENT IN INDIA
—*Dr. L. K. Rao* 109—114

8. GROUND WATER DEPLETION IN SOUTHWEST HARYANA
—*Dr. R.N.Yadav* 115—123

9. CLIMATE CHANGE AND SOCIETY:A GLOBAL PERSPECTIVE
—Dr. M. M. Sheikh, Ravinder Kumar, Mrs. Bipin Mandar 125—136

10. DEGRADATION OF NATURAL VEGETATION IS A BIG HAZARD IN SHEKHAWATI REGION—RAJASTHAN
—Dr. Rajendra Achra 137—145

11. APPLICATION OF REMOTE SENSING AND GIS FOR WATER RESOURCES MANAGEMENT
—Dr.B. C. Jat 147—153

12. ROLE OF VEGETATION - AGRO SYSTEM TO CHECK NATURAL HAZARDS IN THE MOUNTAINS
—S. K. Bandooni and Jagat singh Chaudhary "Junglee" 155—167

13. EL-NINO CAUSES AND IT'S IMPACTS ON ENVIRONMENT
—Dr.S. L. Chopra and Mukesh Kumar Chopra 169—184

14. FLUORIDE TOXICITY AN ALARMING HAZARDS IN DEVELOPING WORLD
—Raaz Maheshwari and Beena Raani 185—199

15. COMMUNITY BASED DISASTER MANAGEMENT
—James E. Robert 201—209

16. DISASTER MANAGEMENT THROUGH REMOTE SENSING AND GIS
—Vikas Tak 211—215

17. DISASTER MANAGEMENT - AN INTEGRATED EFFORT
—Ravinder Kumar and B.C. Jat 217—220

PREFACE

The frequency and severity of natural hazards and disasters have increased in recent years and those trends are expected to continue well into the next century. There is therefore a strong need to strengthen disaster reduction policies around the world to ensure that natural hazards do not result in economic and social disasters.

India is faced with an increasing threat from natural disasters, for reasons of increasing in hazard incidences related to environmental changes, as well as increasing vulnerability of population due to population increasing and socio-economic factors.

The emergence of the information technology sectors in a big way in India has thrown open wide ranging opportunities in of its application in the field of disaster management. Public communication technology can play major role in natural disaster mitigation by making natural disaster mitigation a known concept for general public, i.e. immediate recall and recognition by lay public, and making a difference in individual and collective preparations for meeting disasters.

The main objective of the book 'Natural Hazards and Disaster Management' is to stimulate the communication of solutions to the multidisciplinary problems associated with all spheres of the earth. This book has been compiled by various authers who have been working of the field of geography, geology, oceanography

A natural disaster management campaign could operate from television radio press and the internet simultaneously, Establishment of traditional knowledge base technology. Mitigation programmes should be more effective. Incentive based programmes may be more useful for mitigation than legal imposition. Government grants or subsidies may help to persuade commercial and other institutions to include mitigation measures in their building or reconstruction activities. Trainings and education are very useful tool. Therefore, there is need to train and educate all those involved including disaster management officials, construction specialists and general public. A good public knowledge and understandings of local hazards and vulnerabilities. Public awareness of the mitigation measures which can be applied. Public participation in preparedness programs Better warning system have proved instrumental in evacuating vulnerable groups, moving livestock to safety and mobilizing emergence services and resources.

I express my heartful thanks to Dr. Ramkumar Gurjar assistant Professor,Department of geography University of Rajasthan,Jaipur to encourage me for this work and Dr. B. R. Saini,Vice Principal, Dr.S.B. Shekhawat, Dr. M.L.Gupta ,Dr. Deepak Ahlawat,Dr. Maan singh, senior lecturer, S.N.K.P. Govt. P. G. College, NeemKaThana (Sikar), Rajasthan, who has from time to time guided me .

I am also highly indebted to Prof.B. L. Teli (H.N.B. University,Pauri campus), Prof. Heera Lal Yadav(Gorkhpur), Prof. Hanuman Singh Yadav(Bhopal),Dr. R. B. Singh(Delhi University ,New Delhi) and Dr. R.D. Gurjar (Associate professor and Head) and Dr. S.C. Kalwar, Professor retired, Department of Geography,University of Rajasthan,Jaipur who have helped me in formulating suggestions in many technical aspects.

My thanks are also due to my colleagues Dr. J. N. Gurjar, Shri R. C. Yadav, Shri Hemendara Singh, and Dr. Harish Ola who helped me in getting various informations to be added in this work. Thanks are also due to respected. M. L. Meena, and Dr. R. P. Gurjar, (Lecturer in Geography Govt. College, Kotputali) who helped me in this work.

I would be appreciative of constructive criticism aiming at improvement of the subsequent editions of the book.

DR B. C. JAT

To

My Teacher

Dr. Ramkumar Gurjar

Deparment of Geography

University of Rajasthan, Jaipur

Table 12.6 : List of Vegetation Grown and Found in the Vegetation [illegible] Agro-System at Kot Malla Village, Rudraprayag, Garhwal Himalaya

Type of Vegetation	*Varieties/Species (Names in English/ Hindi/Garhwali)*
Fodder	BANJ/OAK (Quercus incana), BHIMAL (Grewia oppositifolia), KHADIK (Celtis australis), KHAINA (Ficus cunia), TIMLA (Ficus Roxburghii), ROBANIA (Robinia [illegible]), [illegible] (Ficus [illegible]), SAPAR (Quercus [illegible]), KACHNAR (Bauhinia variegata), ONGA (Hovenia dulcis), [illegible] BANJ [illegible], [illegible] (Woodfordia [illegible]), [illegible] (Ficus palmata), [illegible] (Quercus [illegible]), [illegible] (Quercus glauca), [illegible], [illegible] (Desmodium [illegible]), [illegible] (Prunus [illegible]), [illegible] (Celtis [illegible]), [illegible]
Fuel/Timber	CHIR/ PINE (Pinus roxburghii), [illegible] (Pinus [illegible]), KAIL (Pinus wallichiana), DEVDAR (Cedrus deodara), SURAI (Cupressus torulosa), SAGAUN (Tectona grandis), SHISHAM (Dalbergia sissoo), TUNGLA (Rhus parviflora), ASIN (Terminalia tomentosa), ANGU (Fraxinus micrantha), PANGAR (Aesculus indica), ANYAR (Lyonia ovalifolia), TUN (Cedrela toona), RINGAL (Dendrocalamus strictus), BANS (Bambusa arundinacea), BANS CHINA (Phyllostachys [illegible]), BANS PILA (Bambusa vulgaris)

CHAPTER 1

Environmental Hazards and Disaster : Meaning and Concept

DR. D.K. THAKUR

Lecturer, Shri Bhawani Niketan College, Jaipur.

Those events or accidents, whether caused by natural processes or human factors, are called extreme events which occur very rarely and aggravate for human society such as sudden tectonic movements leading to earthquake and volcanic eruption, continued dry conditions leading to prolonged droughts, floods, atmospheric disturbances, collision of celestial bodies etc. *ENVIRONMENTAL HAZARDS* may be defined as those extreme events either natural or man-induced, which exceed the tolerable magnitude within or beyond certain time limits, make adjustment difficult, result in catastrophic losses of property, income and lives and become the headlines of different news media at world level.

Three alternatives or say parallel terms viz., environmental hazards, environmental stresses and environmental disasters are used in one way or the other to deal with the extreme events whether natural or man-induced. A distinction must be drawn between the processes (causal factors) and the responses (results) of extreme events. Hazards are generally taken to the processes, both natural and anthropogenic, which cause an accident/ extreme event or danger whereas 'disaster' is a sudden adverse or unfortunate extreme event which causes great damage to human beings as well as plants and animals. Disasters occur rapidly, instantaneously out that the *ENVIRONMENTAL HAZARDS* are the processes whereas the *ENVIRONMENTAL*

DISASTERS are the results or responses of environmental hazards. It may be mentioned that environmental disasters are always viewed in terms of human beings. The intensity of environmental disasters is weighed in terms of the quantum of damages done to the human society. It is, thus, clear that hazardous environmental processes always create extreme events but not all the extreme events become disasters. These may become disasters only when they adversely affect human society. For example, a very strong tropical cyclone (typhoon), hurricane or tornado becomes only extreme even when it occurs and dies in the midst of an ocean but it becomes disaster when it strikes the inhabited coastal area and inflicts colossal loss to human property and lives. Similarly, a volcanic eruption in uninhabited land or ocean is not extreme but in populated area, it becomes disaster. When the cumulative effects of environmental hazards, environmental disasters and other form of environmental degradation and pollution become so immense that the tolerance limit of the natural environment to assimilate them is surpassed and the environment state of the highly disturbed natural environment is called *ENVIRONMENTAL STRESS.*

It may be further pointed out that to majority of the people environmental hazards and environmental disasters are synonymous terms because these are related to extreme events in one way or the other. The present author, thus, also intends to use these two significant terms of environmental science as synonyms.

Generally, the environmental hazards and disasters are natural and hence these are also termed as *NATURAL HAZARDOUS PROCESSES.* It may be pointed out that the concept and perception of related to their impacts on the organisms in general and mankind in particular. In other words, the natural sudden physical processes and events become hazards and disasters when people live close to a potential danger. For example; if an earthquake of more than 10 on Richter scale occurs in totally uninhabited area it is not a disaster at all but an earthquake even of lower intensity, say below 7 on Richter scale, occurs in heavily populated area, it becomes a severe hazard and disaster. It may be further pointed out that it is not the frequency which makes any extreme event hazardous and disastrous rather it is the intensity, magnitude and dimension and the quantum of damage done by any event which make it hazardous and disastrous. It is also important to note that environmental hazards are not always destructive and disastrous themselves rather it is the effects of these events on other natural processes which become disastrous. For example, the Tajik area of the former southern U.S.S.R. 'is seismically a highly active region, shaken up by direct causalities'. But 'the Tajik earthquake for example, was only of magnitude 5.5, but its timing unfortunately coincided with highly unstable slope conditions caused by height pore-water pressures resulting from snow-melt.' (C. Embleton, 1989) and thus it became disaster.

Types of Environmental Hazards and Disasters

Environmental hazards and disasters are normally divided into two broad categories on the basis of main causative factors viz., *1. NATURAL HAZARDS AND DISASTERS, and (2) MAN-INDUCED HAZARDS AND DISASTERS.* Natural hazards are further sub-divided into two categories e.g., (i) planetary hazards and (ii) extra-terrestrial or extra-planetary hazards and disasters. Planetary hazards and disasters again fall into two subtypes viz., (a) terrestrial or endogenous hazards and (b) atmospheric or exogenous hazards. Man-induced hazards and disasters may be divided into three sub-categories viz., (i) physical (man-induced) hazards (landslides, accelerated soil erosion), (ii) chemical and nuclear hazards and disaster (release of toxic chemical elements in the air, water and soil, sudden outburst of lethal poisonous gases from chemical factories, nuclear explosions and leakage of radioactive elements from nuclear reactor plants etc.) and (iii) biological hazards and disasters (sudden increase or decrease of population of species in a given habitat either due to increased nutrients or increase of toxic chemical elements).

Natural Hazards/Disasters

Natural environmental hazards and disasters involve comparatively rare high intensity processes and extreme events caused by both terrestrial and atmospheric processes. The study of natural hazards/disasters includes the consideration of identification of specific events, finding of their causative factors, assessment of their impacts on human and other biological communities, prediction of such events and finding their remedial measures. Natural hazards and disasters fall into two broad categories e.g. (1) planetary hazards/disasters and (2) extra-planetary or extra-terrestrial natural hazards/disasters.

According to the report of the United Nations Disaster Relief Coordinator (UNDRCO) about 90 per cent of all the reported natural hazards and disasters occur in the developing countries or in the Third World Countries. This observation may not be entirely true because natural disasters do not know any political or economic boundary and consideration. This observation may be because of the fact that most of the developing countries are located in the tropical and subtropical regions of the world where atmospheric processes very often cause numerous natural hazards and disasters such as floods, droughts, forest fires and of course volcanic eruptions and earthquakes wherein the last two are also more prevalent in other parts of the world. Rapid rate of urbanization, industrial expansion, agricultural development, population growth and social development are continuously accelerating the frequency and magnitude of natural hazards and disasters in the developing countries. Developing countries more or less chronically suffer from disaster. In one sense, they live with disaster. The achievements of development programmes have often been destroyed and their future plans halted because funds had to be diverted to relief and recovery activities. It should be noted, however, that a single disaster can strike a nation's social infrastructure, damaging its feed-back system to an irrecoverable extent, (M. Hashizume, 1989).

Table 1.0 : Tabular Classification of Environmental Hazards and Disasters

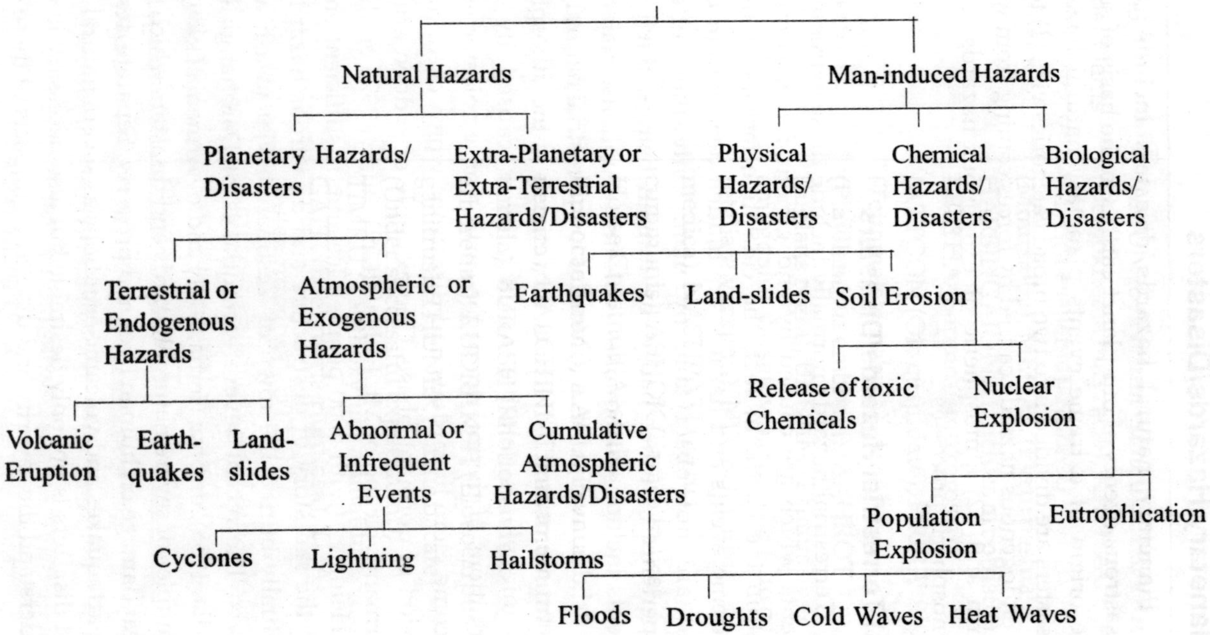

Planetary Hazards/Disasters

Planetary natural hazards/disasters include the most disastrous events of our planet earth. On the basis of sources of the origin of extreme events planetary natural hazards and disasters are divided into two broad categories viz., (1) terrestrial or endogenous hazards caused by forces coming from within the earth and, (2) atmospheric or exogenous hazards caused by atmospheric processes.

(A) Terrestrial Hazards/Disasters

Terrestrial hazards normally include those extreme tectonic events which are caused by end genetic forces coming from within the earth. In fact, the causative factors of terrestrial extreme events and hazards are hidden deep within the earth and are not observable by man. Only their effects are experienced, rather badly, by human beings. Such extreme events include earthquakes, volcanic eruptions, major natural landslides, avalanches etc. Most of the terrestrial natural extreme events are caused by tectonic movements of the lithosphere and oceanic plates relative to each other caused by thermal conditions of the interior of the earth. Those volcanic eruptions become more hazardous and disastrous which occur after long period of dormant phase. One example of sudden eruption of dormant volcano of Mt. Helgafell in January, 1973 on the island of Heimaey (with 5000 people), Iceland, is sufficient enough to tell the sad story of destructive and disastrous hazards which virtually buried the town of Vestmannaeyjar in ash and lava flows. The recent severe earthquakes of Darbhanga in Bihar (India, 1988), or Bhuj (India, 2001) and of Armenia (1989) are the examples of severe natural hazards and disasters which inflicted great damage on human lives and property. Separate description of earthquakes and volcanic eruptions as severe natural hazards and disasters is not only desirable but also necessary in order to understand the severity and disastrous impacts of these extreme events.

Earthquake Hazards/Disasters

An earthquake is a major demonstration of the power of the tectonic forces caused by end genetic thermal conditions of the interior of the earth. 'An earthquake is a motion of the ground surface, ranging from a faint tremor to a wild motion capable of shaking building apart and causing gaping fissures to open in the ground. The earthquake is a form of energy of wave motion transmitted through the surface layer of the earth in widening circles from a point of sudden energy release, the 'focus' (A.N. Strahler and A.H. Strahler, 1976). The magnitude or intensity of energy released by an earthquake is measured by the RICHTER SCALE devised by Charles F. Richter in 1935. The number indicating magnitude or intensity (M) on Richter scale ranges between 0 and 9 but in fact the scale has no upper limit of number because it is a logarithmic scale. 'It is estimated that the total annual energy released by all earthquakes is about 10^{25} ergs, and most of this is from a small number of earthquakes of magnitude over 7' (A.N. Strahler and A.H. Strahler, 1976). The 1934 Bihar earthquake (India) measuring 8.4 magnitude on Richter Scale and Good Friday Earthquake of March 27, 1964, in Alaska, U.S.A. measuring 8.4 to 8.6 on Richter scale may help in assessing the devastation caused by the energy release during earthquakes of varying magnitudes. The world's largest and most intensive recorded earthquake was of the magnitude of 8.9 and the number of recorded earthquakes increase 10 times as magnitude decreases by one.

Richter Scale

Magnitude	*Description*
0	Smallest earth tremor detected by seismograph only. Energy released by such insignificant earthquake amounts to 3×10^{12} ergs.
2.5 to 3.0	Such earthquakes may be felt and detected if they occur near the settlements. The annual frequency of such earthquakes is around 100,000. No damage is done.

4.5	Local damage is done.
5.0	The earthquakes of this magnitude equal in energy to ordinary atomic bomb. The atomic bomb hurled on Hiroshima (Japan) during Second World War equaled the magnitude of 5.7 on Richter Scale. The energy released from such earthquakes equals 8×10^{20} ergs.
6.0	Such earthquakes become destructive within a limited area provided that the geological structure is weak and the area is heavily populated.

Another scale of the measurement of the degrees destructiveness or intensity of earthquakes is *MERCALLI SCALE.* The degree of destructiveness on intensity of an earthquake depends on a variety of factors e.g., magnitude, distance from epicenter, acceleration, duration, amplitude of waves, type of ground-water table, nature of geometries of the region concerned and the nature and type of constructions (such as buildings made of wood or bricks, earthen buildings made of muds, tin shades, huts etc.) affected by an earthquake.

The place of the origin of an earthquake is called FOCUS which is always hidden inside the earth but the depth of which varies from place to place. The deepest earthquake may have its focus at a depth of even 700 km below the ground surface but some of the major Himalayan earthquakes, such as the Bihar-Nepal earthquake of August 21, 1988, have their focus around 20-30 km deep. The place on the grinds surface, which is perpendicular to the buried 'focus' or 'hypocenter', recording the seismic waves for the first time is called ***EPICENTRE.*** The seismic waves move away from the source of the earthquake (focus or hypocentre) in the form of (1) Primary or Pressure waves (P waves), (2) Secondary, Shear or Transverse waves (S waves) and (3) Long waves or surface waves (L waves). These seismic waves are recorded with the help of an instrument called ***SEISMOGRAPH*** *or* ***SEISMOMETER*** at the epicenter. The patterns of recorded seismic waves are studied and various definite information about the centre of the origin of the earthquake (focus or hypocenter), magnitude and destructive power of the earthquake etc., are received.

Magnitude and energy released during an earthquake is generally related to the effects of the earthquake in terms of human beings and his habitats. It is apparent from table that most of the earthquake occurring on the earth are small. On an average about 80,000 earth tremors are recorded by seismographs each year but most of them are not felt by human beings. Beno Guttenburg and Charles F. Richter have stated that the size (magnitude M) and the logarithm of frequency (number of earthquakes N) of earthquakes in a given area of observation are linearly related. On the basis of this analysis one can calculate the probable return periods of earthquakes, of different magnitudes. Great earthquake with magnitudes over 8, generally occur about once every 5 to 10 years. Earthquake of magnitude

Table 1.1 : Magnitudes, Energies, Effects and Frequencies of Earthquakes

S. No.	*Characteristic effect of shocks in populated areas*	*Approximate magnitude (M)*	*Number of earthquakes per year (F)*	*Released energy (ERGS)*
1.	Damages nearly total	≥ 8.0	0.1-0.2	$> 10^{25}$
2.	Great damage	≥ 7.4	4	$\geq 0.4 \times 10^{24}$
3.	Serious damage, rails bent	7.0-7.3	15	$0.04\text{-}0.2 \times 10^{24}$
4.	Considerable damage to buildings	6.2-6.9	100	$0.5\text{-}23 \times 10^{21}$
5.	Slight damage to buildings	5.5-6.1	500	$1\text{-}27 \times 10^{19}$
6.	Felt by all	4.9-5.4	1,400	$3.6\text{-}57 \times 10^{17}$
7.	Felt by many	4.3-4.8	4,800	$1.3\text{-}27 \times 10^{16}$
8.	Felt by some	3.5-4.2	30,000	$1.6\text{-}76 \times 10^{15}$
9.	Not felt but recorded	2.0-3.4	800,000	$4 \times 10^{10}\text{-}9 \times 10^{13}$

8 or more has a probable return period of 50 years in North-East India. Real damages caused by earthquakes begin at magnitude 5 and continue to increase to nearly total destruction in the neighboring settlements by the earthquakes with more than 8 magnitude. Maximum recorded magnitude is 8.9.

Causes of Earthquakes

Earthquakes are caused due to disequilibria in any part of the crust of the earth. A number of causes have been assigned to cause disequilibrium in the earth's crust such as volcanic eruptions, faulting and folding, up warping and down warping, hydrostatic pressure of man-made water bodies like reservoirs and lakes, and of late the plate movements. The occurrence of severe devastating earthquakes of San Fransisco (U.S.A.) in 1906 led H.F. Reid, one of the official investigators of San Fransisco Earthquake Disaster, to advance his important *'ELASTIC REBOUND THEORY'* to explain the mode and causes of earthquakes mainly caused by fractures and faults in the earth's crust and upper mantle. Recently, *PLATE TECTONIC THEORY* has been accepted as the most plausible explanation of earthquakes. As per theory of the plate tectonics the crust of the earth is composed of solid and moving plates having either continental crust or oceanic crust or even both continental-oceanic crust. The earth's crust consists of 6 major plates (Eurasian plate, American plate, African plate, Indian plate, Pacific plate and Antarctic plate) and 20 minor plates. These plates are constantly moving in relation to each other due to thermal convective currents originating deep within the earth. Thus all the tectonic events take place along the margins of plates.

From the standpoint of movement and tectonic events and creation and destruction of geometries the plate margins are divided into three types : (i) *CONSTRUCTIVE PLATE MARGINS* are characterized by continuous addition of geometries from below along the mid-oceanic ridges. These molten hot materials (lavas) are cooled and solidified and are added to the trailing margins of the divergent plates. In fact, divergent plates move in opposite direction from the mid-oceanic ridges and there is always addition of new crust to the trailing ends of these plates because of cooling and solidification of molten lavas. (ii) *DESTRUCTIVE PLATE MARGINS* are those where two convergent plates collide against each other and the heavier plates margin is subducted below the relatively lighter plate margin. This results in constant loss of crustal materials. (iii) *CONSERVATIVE PLATE MARGINS* are those where two plate slip past each other without any collision. This process results neither in the creation nor in the destruction of crust. Major tectonic events associated with these plate margins are rupture and faults along the constructive plate margins; faulting and folding along the destructive plate margins and transform faults along the conservative plate margins. Thus these major tectonic events of faulting and folding and mountain building cause volcanic eruptions and earthquakes of varying magnitudes along different plate margins.

Normally, moderate earthquakes are caused along the constructive or divergent plate margins because the rate of rupture of the crust and consequent movement of plates away from the mid-oceanic ridges is rather slow and the rate of upwelling of lavas is also slow. Consequently, shallow focus earthquakes are caused along the constructive plate margins or say along the mid-oceanic ridges. The depth of focus of the earthquake associated with the constructive plate margins ranges between 25 km to have occurred at the depth of 60 km. It is thus obvious that the earthquake occurring along the mid-Atlantic Ridge, mid-Indian oceanic Ridge and East Pacific Rise are caused because of movement of plates in opposite directions (divergence) and consequent formation of faults and upwelling of magma (say Vulcanicity, more specifically fissure flow).

Earthquakes of high magnitudes and deep focus are caused along the convergent or destructive plate margins because of collision of two convergent plates and consequent subduction of one plate margin along the Benioff zone. Here mountain building, faulting and violent volcanic eruptions (central eruptions) causes disastrous earthquakes having the focus at the depth upto 700 km. The earthquakes having their focus upto 720 km depth have been recorded so far. This process, convergence of plates and related plate collision, explains the maximum occurrence of earthquakes of varying magnitudes along the *FIRY RING OF THE PACIFIC or CIRCUM PACIFIC BELT* (along the western and eastern margins of the Pacific ocean or say along the western coastal margins of North and South America and thus the Rockies-Andes, mountain belt and along the eastern coastal margins of Asia and Island areas and festoons parallel to Asiatic coast) and *MID-CONTINENTAL BELT* (along the Alpine-Himalayan Chains). The earthquakes of the western marginal areas of North and South America are caused because of subduction of American plate below the Pacific plate and resultant tectonic forces whereas the earthquakes of the eastern margins of Asia are originated because of subduction of Pacific plate under the Asiatic plate. Similarly, the subduction of African plate below Asiatic plate cause earthquakes of the mid-continental belt. Creation of transform faults along the conservative plate margins explains the occurrence of severe earthquakes of California (U.S.A.). Here one part of California moves north-eastward while the other part moves south-westward along the fault plane and thus is formed transform fault which causes earthquakes.

Distribution of Earthquakes

The world map of the distribution of earthquakes prepared by the seismologists on the basis of computer analysis and simulation of 30,000 earthquakes that occurred between 1961 and 1967 very much coincides with the traditional map of world distribution of earthquakes viz., (i) Circum Pacific Belt or Ring of Fire surrounding the Pacific Ocean, (ii) Mid-Continental Belt representing epicentres located along the Alpine Himalayan chains of Eurasia and northern Africa and epicentres of east African fault zone and (iii) Mid-Atlantic Belt representing the earthquakes located along the mid-Atlantic Ridge and its offshoots. "The high-quality seismicity maps showed that narrow belts of epicenters coincide almost exactly with the crest of mid-Atlantic (Ridge), the east Pacific, and other oceanic ridges, where plates separate. Earthquake epicenters are also aligned along transform faults, where plates slide past each other. But earthquakes that occur at depths greater than about 100 kilometers (60 miles) typically occur near margins where plates collide. It is a basic tenet of the theory of plate tectonics that these deep earthquakes actually define the positions of subducted places which are plunging back into the mantle beneath an overriding plate' (F. Press and R. Sever, 1978). It may be pointed out that the occurrences of earthquakes along the plate margins (boundaries) are well explained on the basis of plate tectonic theory but the earthquakes originating within the plates are difficult to be explained on the basis of this revolutionary theory. For example, the earthquakes of New Madrid, Missouri (U.S.A., 1812), Charleston, South Carolina (U.S.A., 1886), Boston, Massachusetts (U.S.A., 1755), Tang-Shan (China, 1976), Koyna (December 11, 1967, India) etc., are a few examples on intraplate earthquakes. Similarly, 'the seismicity of the Indian Shield as revealed from Kutch (1819), Koyna (1967), Bhadrachalam (1969) and Broach (1970) cannot be explained easily by plate tectonics since they occurred far away from the plate boundary' (J.G. Negi, in the Hindu, September 18, 1988).

The earthquakes in India along the Himalayas and foothill zones may be explained in terms of plate tectonics. The Asiatic plate is moving southward whereas the Indian plate is moving northward and hence the northern margin of the Indian plate is being subducted below the Asiatic plate. This collision of Asiatic and Indian plates and subduction of Indian plate and consequent folding and faulting and gradual rise of the Himalayas at the rate of 50 mm per year cause earthquakes of northern India, Tibet and Nepal. According to J.G. Negi, P.K. Agarwal and O.P. Pandey (as reported in the Hindu, September 18, 1988) 'the Indian subcontinent has deformed at places due to the Indian Ocean floor spreading process. India folds at places and when the energy reaches the elastic limit, the rocks breakup and trigger strike-slip and thrust fault earthquakes. The Himalayan fault zone is not actually one fault but a broad system of interactive faults. It consists of a complex grid of faults extending all along this colliding zone. The earthquake belt extends from Sulaiman and Kirthar shear zones in the west, the Himalayas in the north and Burmese arc in the east'. These tectonic events caused by plate movements cause earthquakes in the northern and north-eastern parts of India.

Hazardous Effects of Earthquakes

It may be restated that the intensity of earthquakes and their hazardous impacts are determined not on the basis of the magnitude of seismic intensity as determined by *RICHTER or MERCALLI* scales but are decided on the basis of quantum of damages done by a specific earthquakes to human lives and property. An earthquake becomes hazard or disaster only when it strikes the populated area. Sometimes the moderate earthquakes on Richter scale inflict great damages by stimulating and augmenting other natural physical processes such as landslides, floods and fire. Thus it is obvious that it is not necessary that an earthquake creates havoc itself but it also becomes disastrous indirectly. The direct and indirect disastrous effect of earthquakes include deformation of ground surfaces, damages and destruction of human structures such as buildings, rails, roads, bridges, dams, factories, destruction of towns and cities, loss of human and animal lives and property, violent fires, landslides, floods, disturbance in groundwater conditions etc.

(*i*) **Slope Instability and Failures and Landslides**-The shocks produced by earthquakes particularly in those hilly and mountainous areas which are composed of weaker ideologies and are tectonically sensitive and weak cause slope instability and slope failure and ultimately cause landslides and debris falls which damage settlements and transport systems on the lower slope segments. The Peruvian earthquake of May, 1970 tells the awesome story disastrous tragedy inflicted by the said earthquake to the town of Youngay. The shocks generated by strong earthquake in May, 1970 triggered off the collapse of ice cap seated on the peak of high mountain called Huascaran of 6654 m height near the town of Youngay in Peru. Huge masses of falling ice dislodged thousands of tonnes of rock mass from the said mountain and thus was generated a gigantic debris flows down the slope of Huascaran mountain travelling at the speed of 320 kilometers per hour. The volume of debris flows further increased down the slope because more and more debris and water joined the main debris flow route. This enormous mass of debris flow covered a distance of 15 kilometres within few minutes. The enormity of the mass of debris may be gauged from the fact that individual rock blocks measured about 15 cubic metres. This enormous debris falls triggered by earthquake buried many buildings and human structures of Yungay town and killed about 25,000 people.

The second example of slope failure and resulted landslides caused by earthquakes may be cited from the Tajik earthquake of 1989. "The Tajik earthquake in the south of the former USSR on 21 January, 1989, for example, was only of magnitude of 5.5, but its timing unfortunately coincided with highly unstable slope conditions cause by high pore-water pressure resulting from snow-melt. Huge landslides and rivers of mud 20 m deep were set off that engulfed houses and even whole villages. This is seismically a highly active region, shaken by upwards of 3000 tremors a year, but these cause few direct casualities-it is the effects on other natural processes that are disastrous' (C. Embleton, 1989, in Aerospace Survey and Natural Disaster Reduction, ITC, Enschede, Netherlands, 1989).

The occurrence of earthquakes during wet season in the hilly and mountainous regions causes landslides even if the earthquakes are of very moderate nature. This is the reason that people notice earth tremors through landslides during wet season but fail to notice such earth tremors during dry season of the year. 'Landslides are often triggered by earthquakes in mountainous zones, especially in the wet season. I was baffled once when a farmer in southern Italy asked me 'why do earthquakes always occur in winter? Until I realized that earthquakes occurring during the dry summers, when most slopes are stable, may hardly be noticed by the peasants' (H.T.Verstappen, 1989, in Aerospace Survey and Natural Disaster Reduction, ITC, Enschede, Netherlands, 1989).

(*ii*) **Damage to Human Structures-**Earthquakes inflict great damage to human structures such as building, roads, rails, factories, dams, bridges and thus cause heavy loss of human property. In fact the principal damage emanating from earthquake disaster is construction failure. It may be pointed out that extent of damage done to the human structures not only depends on intensity and magnitude of earthquakes but also on the characteristics of ground upon which the buildings are constructed and the nature of materials of which the buildings have been constructed (such as stones, bricks, muds, concrete, cement, tins, huts etc.). It may be stated that in the ground surface composed of unconsolidated geomaterials such as alluvium, colluvium, artificially filled up and levelled up depressions, swamp deposits reclaimed through the dumping of coarse sand and city garbages and vibrations of earthquakes last longer and the amplitudes of seismic waves are greater than in the structure of consolidated materials and bedrocks. Thus the earthquakes cause more damage in the areas of unconsolidated ground that their counterparts in the regions of solid structures and bedrocks.

Two major earthquakes of Bihar (India)-Nepal border in 1934 and 1988 explain the impact of earthquakes disasters on human structures and human lives. It was the afternoon of 15th January 1934 when a powerful earthquake of the magnitude (M) 8.4, one of the greatest seismic events of the world, struck the northern Bihar plain (a part of the Ganga plain) and the Himalayan country of Nepal and adjoining Tibet. The epicenter of the earthquake was located at 26.6^0 N and 86.8^0 E (near Darbhanga in Bihar, India). The damages caused by this disastrous earthquakes in India (Bihar), Nepal and Tibet include

10700 human deaths, landslides and slumping in an area of 250 km length and 60 km width, ruptures in the ground surface, faults etc., which caused irreparable damage to human structure. This area remained more or less seismically dormant (as regards severe earthquakes only) except ordinary earth tremors for more than 54 years but was suddenly struck by devastating hazardous earthquake in the morning hour of August 21, 1988. 'Once again the epicenter was located near Darbhanga town (toward Bihar-Nepal border) and the focus may lie 20-30 km deep at the intersection of Patna fault (or nearby parallel fault) and Himalayan frontal thrust. The seismic energy of the 1988 earthquake (6.5 magnitude on Richter scale) was 1000 times smaller than the great earthquake of 1936 (with magnitude of 8.4 on Richter scale as referred to above) but more than 850 people were killed, thousand injured in India and Nepal, with an earth surface split up at many places and more than 25000 houses damaged. The damage is high (inspite of comparatively lower magnitude of 6.5 than the higher magnitude of 8.4 in 1934 Bihar earthquake) due to the location of the affected area in the unconsolidated Gangetic alluvium which acts like a seismic amplifier' (J.G. Negi, 1988, in the Hindu, September 18, 1988). It may be pointed out that a fortnight ago the North-Eastern India was rocked by more severe earthquake (magnitude being 7.3 on Richter scale, epicenter being near Imphal, Manipur, India) on August 6, 1988 but the damage was insignificant because of the fact that ground materials of N-E India are consolidated. Many of the houses damaged in Bihar because of Darbhanga earthquake of 1988 were quite old and constructed by bricks and muds.

The recent example of severe hazardous earthquake of Mexico city on September 1985 tells the story of disastrous effects of seismic hazards on human structures and property. Though the epicentre was located about 400 km south-west of Mexico city, the capital of Mexico, but greatest damage was caused in Mexico city. It is believed to be the strongest earthquake in Latin America in last 100 years or so. The total destruction caused by this earthquake includes death toll 10,000; missing people 2000; injured people 40,000; building collapsed 400; building severely damaged 6000; moderately damaged building 500,000; total loss of property 4000 million US dollars; loss of Gross National Product (GNP) 136 billion US dollars. Besides, the infrastructures of the city were seriously damaged, for example, water pipes were broken, telecommunication lines and systems were severely damaged, power and water supplies were disrupted, inner vehicular transportation was badly effected.

Table 1.2 : Major Earthquake Hazards of India

Time	*Location*	*Effects*
October 11, 1737	Calcutta	3,00,000 people were killed, the worst earthquake of India in its seismic history.
September 1, 1793	Mathura	Adversely affected larger areas including Garhwal, Kumaun and Shimla hills.
June 16, 1819	Kutch	2,000 people were killed, bhuj city was destroyed, famous mosque of 15th Century in Ahmedabad city had broken down, rise of land in a length of 15 km in the Rann of Kutch known as Allah Bund.
June 16, 1828	Kashmir	1,000 people were killed.
August 26, 1833	Bihar	Adversely affected the areas from Bihar to Nepal; 1000 houses were destroyed.
February 19, 1842	Jalalabad	Adversely affected the areas from Delhi (India) to Kabul city of Afghanistan.
April 1, 1843	Deccan India	Carnool, Solapur, Belgaon and Bellary cities greatly damaged.
January 10, 1869	Assam	Adversely affected a large area of 2,50,000 square miles.
May 30, 1885	Kashmir	3,000 people were killed.

July 14, 1886	Dhaka (Bangladesh) & W. Bengal	Adversely affected large area of West and East Bengal, Assam, Sikkim, Bhutan and Chotanagpur covering an area of 2,30,000 square miles.
June 12, 1887 (8.7)	Shillong (Meghalaya)	1500 people were killed, houses even made up of stones in the cities of Naogaon, Shillong, Gauhati (Guwahati), Golpara etc., heavily damaged and destroyed; affected area was about 17,50,0000 square miles, a great fault of 35 feet width and 12 miles length formed in the ground.
June 15, 1890	Kutch	1500 people were killed.
April 4, 1905 (8.6)	Kangra	20,000 people were killed, whole Punjab was badly affected.
July 3, 1990	Assam (Dhubri)	Dhubri town was destroyed.
January 5, 1934	Bihar-Nepal	8.4 magnitude on Richter Scale; 10700 people were killed.
August, 15, 1950 (8.7)	Assam	1500 people were killed; 60 died after shocks; floods in the rivers of Assam.
December 11, 1967 (6.5)	Koyna (Satara)	1000 people were killed; 2063 wounded and 10,000 homeless.
August 21, 1988	Darbhanga (Bihar)-Nepal	Magnitude 6.7on Richter scale, 850 people were killed.

Yet another example of earthquake of moderate nature but of serious consequences was recorded at 6 A.M. on February 9, 1971 in the San Fernando Valley, located to the north-west of Los Angeles (U.S.A.). Though the earthquake lasted only for 60 seconds but this too caused deaths of 64 persons. The greatest impact of this earthquake on the Los Angeles community was the realization of the need of urban planning in view of the seismic events as the toll in human lives and the severe structural effects of the San Fernando Earthquake shocked the entire Los Angeles community into renewed awareness for the need for urban planning to minimize or forestall the damaging effects of major earthquake' (A.N. Strahler, 1978). Although the earthquake was of the magnitude of only 6.5 on Richter scale but it caused severe damages to standing buildings. For example, the collapse of Olive New Hospital in Sylmar shocked every body because this building was constructed in conformity with the earthquake resistant standards. 'Fortunately the ground shaking was of a brief duration; had it persisted for a longer time structural damages would have been much more severe than it was' (A.N. Strahler, 1978).

(*iii*) **Damages to the Towns and Cities-** Earthquake have their worst effects on buildings and large agglomerations of human population. The earth tremors of higher magnitudes shake the ground to such an extent that the large building collapse and men and women are buried under the large debris and rubbles of collapsed structural materials of buildings, groundwater pipes are bent and damaged and thus water supply is totally disrupted, electric and telephone wires and cables are heavily damaged causing total disruption of electric supply and telecommunication systems, obstruction and destruction of sewer systems causes epidemics, road blocks throw the transport system out of gear etc. Calcutta city was severely damaged due to severe earthquake of October 11, 1737 as thousands of building were severely damaged and 3,00,000 people were killed. Nearly 2,00,000 people were killed within a period of 100 years due to earthquakes of 1688, 1693 and 1783. The sad tale of the destruction of Mexico city due to 1985 earthquake has already been described above.

(*iv*) **Loss of Human Lives and Property-**The destructiveness of an earthquake is determined on the basis of human casualties in terms of deaths. Some of the world's worst earthquake in terms of human deaths during 19th century, first half of 20th century and in the later half of the 20th century have been listed in and severe hazardous earthquakes causing heavy toll of human lives during the 20th century have been shown. It is apparent from that it is not the magnitude (intensity) of earthquake alone which matters more as regards the human casualties but it is the density of human population and houses which matter more in term of human deaths and loss of property. For example, the Kangra earthquake of India in 1905 recorded 8.6 magnitude on Richter scale but it could cause death of only 20,000 persons whereas in 1976 Tang-shan earthquake of China measuring 7.8 to 8.1 on Richter scale caused deaths of 750,000 people. From the standpoint of human deaths between 20,000 persons and 50,000 persons occurred in 1971 (earthquake of west-central China, death toll, 20,000 persons), 1293 in Kamakura, Japan (22,000 deaths), 1731 in Peking, China (22,000 deaths), 1556 in Shen-Shu, China (25,000 deaths), 1988 in Armenia (26,000 deaths), 1896 in Sanriku, Japan (27,000 deaths), 1828 in Honshu, Japan (30,000 deaths), 1847 in Zenkoji, Japan (34,000 deaths), 1755 in Northern Persia (40,000 deaths), 1939 in Chile (40,000 deaths), 1939 in Erzincan, Turkey (40,000 deaths), 1797 in Quito, Ecuador (41,000 deaths), 1856 in Corinth, Greece (45,000 deaths), 1783 in Calabria, Italy (50,000 deaths).

Earthquake Hazards in India

India is frequently adversely affected by moderate to severe earthquakes in different parts of the country mainly the Himalayan regions, north Bihar, N.E. India, Gujarat etc. After first shocking earthquake of Koyna in 1967 in Maharashtra, India has been severely rocked in August, 1988 (Darbhanga earthquake, 6.7), October, 1991 (Uttarkashi, Uttaranchal, 6.6), September, 1993 (Latur, Maharashtra, 6.3), May, 1997 (Jabalpur, M.P., 6.0), March, 1999 (Chamoli, Uttaranchal, 6.8), January, 2001 (Bhuj, Gujarat, 8.1) etc.

On the basis of magnitude of damage risk, India is divided into five damage risk zones. 1. **Zone I of least damage risk** includes the places of some parts of Punjab and Haryana, plain areas of Uttar Pradesh, portions of plains of north Bihar and West Bengal, delta areas of the Godavari, coastal plain areas of the Godavari, coastal plain areas of Maharashtra and Kerala, desert areas of Rajasthan and most areas of Gujarat except Kutch region. 2. **Zone II of low damages risk,** includes southern Punjab and Haryana, southern parts of plains of Uttar Pradesh, eastern Rajasthan, coastal districts of Orissa, Tamil Nadu etc. 3. **Zone III of Moderate damage risk** represents the areas of southern and south-eastern Rajasthan, most of Madhya Pradesh, Maharashtra and Karnataka, Southern Bihar, Northern and north-western orissa etc. 4. **Zone IV of high damage risk** covers Jammu and Kashmir, Himachal Pradesh, northern Punjab and Haryana, Delhi, western Uttar Pradesh, 'Tarai' and 'Bhabar' regions and Himalayan regions of Uttaranchal and Bihar, and Sikkim areas. 5. **Zone V of very high damage risk** includes parts of Jammu and Kashmir, some parts of Himachal Pradesh, Uttaranchal, extreme north Bihar, entire north-eastern India and Kutch region of Gujarat.

Though the plains of West Bengal comes under the zone of least damage risk but the devastating severe earthquake of Kolkata on 11 October, 1737 killing 300,000 people put a question mark against this concept. The zone of very high damage risk of Kutch region of Gujarat registered most devastating killer earthquake on January 26, 2001 (8.1 on Richter scale) in its seismic history of past 180 year killing 50,000 to 100,000 people. The towns of Bhuj, Anjar and Bhachau were flattened and razed to the ground.

Killer Bhuj Earthquake (Jan. 26, 2001)-While the people of India were celebrating the first republic day on January 26, 2001 of the new century in different parts of the country and the might of armed forces of the country was being displayed in New Delhi, the nature demonstrated its might by unleashing its immense energy in the form of a very severe earthquake which rocked Kutch region at 8.45 A.M. and shook the region for almost a minute. Within no time the village and towns were flattened, high rise buildings collapsed, many villages and towns became heaps of debris, communication and power lines were completely disrupted, transport system was thrown out of gear and settlements became ruin. This was the second most devastating earthquake in the earthquake history of India after 1737 killer earthquake of Kolkata when 300,000 people were killed. The epicenter was located near Bhuj town (population 150,000). A moderate quake measuring 4.20 on Richter scale was registered on 24 December, 2000 the epicenter of this precursor quake was located only 22 km away from Bhuj town but no attention was paid to this precursor seismic event either by experts or govt. agencies. The Bhuj quake of Jan. 26, 2001 was measured 6.9 on Richter scale by the Indian Meteorological Department (IMD) while the quake was measured 7.9 which was subsequently upgraded to 8.1 by the USA, France and China. National Geophysical Research Institute (NGRI) of India and Bhabha Atomic Research Center (BARC) also confirmed the American measurement (8.1) According to Indian Meteorological Department the main reason for the difference in the magnitude of the quake was the application of different methodologies for the measurement of seismic magnitude by different countries and organizations. It may be pointed out that the IMD uses body wave for the measurement of seismic magnitude while the USA uses shock waves for this. This severe devastating earthquake claimed the lives of 50,000 to 100,000 people and adversely affected 5,00,000 people. Bhuj, Bhachau and Anjar town were flattened, most of the buildings collapsed, 90, 60 and 50 per cent houses collapsed in Bhuj, Rajkot and Ahmedabad respectively.

If we look at the past seismic history of Gujarat, it appears that a severe earthquake occurs every 30 years e.g. Bhawnagar earthquake, 1872; Kutch earthquake, 1903; Dwarka earthquake, 1940; Broach earthquake, 1970 and Bhuj earthquake, 2001. Between 1845 and 1956, sixty six moderate earthquakes were registered in Kutch area but no one was killed, 5 severe and one very severe earthquakes rocked the area. In fact, the sequence of destruction of Kutch began with the severe earthquake of June 19, 1819 (7.1 on Richter scale) when 2000 people were killed, Bhuj town was destroyed, famous mosque of Ahmedabad was damaged, a 100 km ridge known as Allah Bund (most of which is now in Sindh of Pakistan, only 15 km ridge in India) was created.

The main reasons for the recent Bhuj quake of 2001 were : seafloor spreading of Indian Ocean at the rate of 5 cm per year, gradual northward movement of Indian plate and reactivated faults below the ground surface. Two major connecting faults have been located in Kutch region. A 200 km long and 100 km wide fault runs east-west between Bhuj and Ahmedabad. The second fault measuring 500 km in length and 100 km in width runs in north-south direction through Ahmedabad, Mehsana and Baroda and is known as Combay Graben. These sub-terranean faults intersect each other near Viramgam, Santhal pur and Radhampur towns and become the pivot of seismic events whenever these are activated due to plate movement.

Atmospheric or Exogenous Hazards

The atmospheric hazards are related to weather and climatic extreme events. The atmospheric environmental natural hazards are caused by atmospheric processes which originate from within the atmosphere and hence these natural hazards are also called as Exogenous Natural Hazards. The extreme weather and climatic events may be divided into two groups viz., (a) abnormal and infrequent events (lasting for very short time such as tropical cyclones (typhoons, tornadoes and hurricanes), severe lightning and fires and (b) the events which prevail for prolonged period of time. Such events become hazards through cumulative effects such as droughts and floods, heatwaves, cold waves etc.

Tropical Cyclones and Local Storms

Tropical cyclone, representing closed low pressure system generally having a diameter of about 650 kilometres, is one of the most powerful, destructive, dangerous and deadly atmospheric storms on the planet earth. Tropical cyclones are variously called in different parts of the globe as *HURRICANES* in the north

Atlantic Ocean (mainly in the Caribbean Sea and south-eastern U.S.A.), *TYPHOONS* in the North Pacific Ocean (mainly in China Sea, eastern and southern coasts of China, Japan, Philippines and south-east Asia), *CYCLONES* in Bangladesh and eastern coastal areas of India and *'WILLY WILLY'* in Australia.

Tropical cyclones become more disastrous natural hazards because of their high wind speed of 180 to 400 kilometres per hour, high tidal surges, high rainfall intensity (highest recorded rainfall value exceeded 2000 mm per day in Philippines), very low atmospheric pressures causing unusual rise in sea level, and their persistence for several days or say about one week. The total cumulative effects of high velocities of wind, torrential rainfall and transgression of sea water into the coastal land become so enormous that the cyclones cause havoc in the affected areas and thus tremendous loss of human lives and property is the ultimate result of such atmospheric delug. The 'storm surge' or 'tidal surge' referees to unusual rise in sea level caused by very low atmospheric pressure and the stress of the strong gusty winds on the sea surface. These storm surges or tidal surges, when coincide with high tide, are further intensified and after intruding into the coastal land cause widespread inundation of coastal areas and great damage of human lives and property. The following case histories of a few most powerful and disastrous tropical cyclones may unravel the magnitude of destructions wrought by these natural atmospheric disturbances.

(1) CYCLONIC hazards very often visit the eastern coastal areas of India and the southern coastal areas of Bangladesh. The disaster of the deadliest storm in the recorded history occurred on November 12, 1970 in the coastal lowland of Bangladesh. This Bay of Bengal disastrous cyclone tells the magnitude of environmental hazards in respect of its killer impact on the affected people as it caused as many as 300,000 deaths (some sources put the figure between 300,000 and 1,000,000 deaths in Bangladesh and West Bengal of India) wherein most of the deaths were caused by drawing in the stomp surge of oceanic water (20 feet)

on the land. The official record of Bangladesh presented the total loss as death of people-200,000, missing persons-50,000 to 100,000, cattle death-300,000, houses destroyed-40,000, crops losses of 63,000,000 US dollars, fishing boats destroyed-9000 (offshore) and 90,000 (inland water).

The tropical cyclones coming from over the Bay of Bengal also become hazardous to the east coastal lands of India (West Bengal, Orissa, Andhra Pradesh and Tamil Nadu). The deadliest hazardous cyclone struck the east coast in 1737 and claimed the lives of 300,000 people. Other disastrous cyclones occurred in 1977 (55,000 deaths), 1864 (50,000 deaths), 1839 (20,000 deaths) etc. The November, 1977 cyclonic storm struck Andhra coast and generated three successive 'storm surges' of which the biggest surge of 6m height was recorded in the last. This deadly storm moved with a speed of 175 kilometres per hour. The biggest surge raced into the coastal low lying areas up to 20 kilometres inland and thus killed 55,000 inhabitants through drowning caused by sudden inundation, destroyed the homes of 2,000,000 people, ruined 1,200,000 hectares of agricultural crops and made most of the coastal land barren and wasteland because of deposition of thick layer of salt on the soils by storm surges. The saline land could be reclaimed only after three years.

The strongest and most notorious cyclone hit the Andhra coast on May 9, 1990. It was 25 times stronger and more disastrous than the deadliest cyclone of November 1977 (which also struck the Andhra coast as referred to above) but could claim the lives of only 598 people (official figure but the actual figure might have crossed 1000 deaths). Beside killing 598 people, it adversely affected 3,000,000 people, rendered 300,000 people homeless, perished 90,000 cattle and caused loss of 1000 crore rupees worth of property. Very low figure of human causalities (598 deaths) inspite of 25 times more intensity of May, 1990 cyclone than the latter was particularly because of the advance monitoring and prediction of the cyclone from the time of its formation in the Bay of Bengal off the southern coast of Tamil Nadu on May 5, 1990.

This cyclone is termed most notorious in the sense it shifted its course almost by 90 degree. But more than 100 direct warning system and even dying INSAT-IB provided direct audio-broadcasts from meteorological stations in Chennai and Hyderabad and 6 cyclone detection radars fitted all along the coastline provided minute by minute information about the movement of incoming cyclone. Initially, the cyclone was moving westward and was expected to strike the southern coast of Tamil Nadu near Nagapattinam but after May 6 it suddenly shifted its course northwards and eventually hit the coastal districts of Andhra Pradesh and unleased the devastating force of its fury on five districts viz., Krishna, Guntur, East Godavari West Godavari and Visakhapatnam. It may be pointed out that the cyclone was so strong and enormous that some of the major towns of Krishna and Guntur districts such as Vijayawada, Machlipatnam, Pamarru, Guntur, Bapatia, Repalle and Tenali, which could not be affected by the deadliest 1977 cyclone and tidal wave, were also hit this time by the powerful storm surges (tidal waves) caused by *GALE* winds with a speed of 220 to 250 kilometres per hour.

Super Cyclone of Orissa, 1999

The 29th October, 1999 proved a black and killer day for the inhabitants of the coastal region of Orissa (India) when the strongest cyclone in the cyclone history of India struck the Orissa coast and caused a havoc of mass destruction through its notorious acts from October 29 to 31, 1999. Nearly one-third of Orissa plunged into gloom and despair. Prior to the final assault by this killer cyclone, a strong cyclone already knocked at the door of Orissa on October 18, 1999 with a velocity of 200 km per hour. This cyclone claimed the lives of 200 people, damaged 460 villages and adversely affected 5,00,000 people in Ganjam district. The people of Orissa were yet to recover from the trauma of this cyclone, the killer super cyclone hit the Orissa coast on October 29. The successive phases of the formation and advancement of super cyclone may be outlined as follows :

(1) **October 25 :** A depression was formed 500 km east of Portblair in Andaman, sea, which started to move in N-W direction from the midnight and soon turned into a deep depression. **(2) October 26 :** The deep depression changed into a cyclonic storm by the morning of October 26 which was stationed about 350 km away from Portblair. The Indian Meteorological Department started to issue warning of advancing cyclonic storm. **(3) October 27 :** By the morning of October 27, this cyclonic storm changed to severe cyclonic storm and was positioned 750 km away from Paradeep port. It remained stationary for 6 hours at the distance of 600 km from Paradeep. **(4) October 28 :** Advancing towards north-west this severe cyclonic storm became a fully developed super cyclonic storm and moved towards Paradeep with a velocity of 260 km. **(5) October, 29 :** Indian Meteorological Department (IMD) issued an alarm of warning about the arrival of the super cyclone between Paradeep and Puri. Though the Govt. of Orissa was posted with this warning by 5.30 AM but this warning could not be conveyed to the general public due to lack of radio network.

Ultimately, the super cyclone entered Orissa on October 29, 1999 and began to play its game of destruction in 10 coastal districts. Moving with a velocity of 300 km per hour the cyclone became stationary for 8 hours over this vast area. This disastrous cyclone generated 9 m high tidal surges which transgressed upto 15-20 km inside coastal region. Kendrapara, Jagatsinghpur, Balosore, Paradeep, Bhadrak and Khuda were worst affected. According to official sources more than ten thousand people were killed and 200 villages were completely washed out but the unofficial sources put human death toll at about hundred thousand. More than 6000 people were killed in Jagatsinghpur alone. Several hundred thousand cattle perished and countless people were rendered homeless. The standing kharif crops over 1.75 million hectares were destroyed. The loss of property mounted to about 10,000 crore rupees (1000 billion rupees). The severe super cyclonic storm resulted into the disruption of the supply of water and electricity. The communication system was thrown out of gear. Destruction and obstruction of roads and rails brought a grinding halt to rail and road transport which continued for weeks. Thousands of families suffered from mental agony due to separation of their kith and kins. Paradeep port was greatly damaged that it became uncoperational for weeks. Most of the trees were uprooted. Surface and ground water were so greatly polluted due to dead bodies (both human and animal) that it became unsuitable for domestic uses and gave birth to the outbreak of epidemic. Though the cyclone vanished by October 31 but it left behind the ugly scene of destruction and tragedy of epidemic, hunger and pollution which broke the backbone of already poor inhabitants.

The northern part of the Bay of Bengal mostly the Ganga Delta plains of West Bengal, India and Bangladesh very often suffers from frequent severe cyclonic storms and resultant storm surges (tidal waves) because of a combination of several natural conditions and phenomena such as large astronomical tides, funneling coast configuration (spread of land from three sides in arcade shape, forming the head of Bay of Bengal), low and flat terrains of coastal area and frequent occurrence of severe cyclonic storms. About 12 to 13 tropical cyclones with wind speed below 63 kilometres per hour occur every year in the northern Bay of Bengal. About 5 of these tropical cyclones becomes strong and severe with average wind speed of more than 63 kilometres per hour. The recurrence interval of disastrous cyclone is every five years.

(2) HURRICANES very often strike the southern and the south-eastern coasts of the USA, Gulf coasts of Louisiana, Taxas, Alabama and Florida are worst affected areas. The Galveston, Texas (USA) disaster of September 8, 1900 tells the story of devastation caused by hurricanes in the Gulf coastal regions of the U.S.A. The terrible hurricane generated a strong storm surge (tidal wave) which raced inland and killed 6000 people mostly through drowning caused by inhumation under 10 to 15 feet (3 to 4.5m) deep water and destroyed 3000 houses. Flying planks

and timbers under the force of strong gale winds also caused several deaths and damages to human structures.

It may be pointed out that Mississippi Delta Plains of the state of Louisiana (U.S.A.) have the equivalence of Ganga Delta Plains of India and Bangladesh as regards the frequency and intensity of tropical cyclones but the damages mainly in the form of human causalities are far less in the former than in the latter because of more advanced and better warning systems. The Audrey Hurricane of June, 1957 struck the Louisiana coast between New Orleans and Galveston. Though the storm was very severe as it smashed houses and floated them away, uprooted sealed concrete tombs and floated them 32 kilometres away from their resting places, but only 550 human deaths could be caused because of better warning systems and spontaneous response of people to the warning and predictions. In fact the water level used to rise at the rate of 1.5 feet per hour. Thus most of the people had ample time to evacuate them to safer places before the water level forced by strong storm surge could reach its peak of 8 to 12 feet (2.4 to 3.6 m) above high tide water.

(3) TRACY CYCLONE struck Darwin city of Australia (a coastal city of the Northern Territory) on the Christmas Day of 1974 and caused deaths of 49 persons and left 16 people missing. Though the Tracy storm was small as the diameter of the area of gale force winds (above 63 kilometres per hour) way only about 100 kilometres but it was certainly an intense storm as its destructive intensity was concerned. The destructiveness of the storm surge caused by this cyclone was minimised because of the fact that it occurred during a period of neap tides inspite of reduction in the intensity the Tracy cyclone damaged 80 per cent of the buildings of Darwin city having a population of 45000 people at that time (1974), caused total disruption of power supply thus plunging the entire city into darkness, put all the services of water and power supply, sanitation, transport and communication out of gear. There is little doubt that the relatively very small loss of life in Darwin (city) can be attributed to the fact that the cyclone was accompanied by a restricted

storm surge effect; major damage was produced by high winds and torrential rain. Nevertheless, the problems encountered in Darwin, serve to highlight the magnitude of the tropical cyclone danger in much more densely populated areas of developing rather than developed countries' (J.E. Hobbs, 1980).

(4) LOCAL STORMS-The severe local storms of hazardous nature include TORNADOES (which affect the southern and the eastern USA) and thunderstorms. Tornadoes, though smallest in area of all the hazardous atmospheric storms, are very deadly to human lives and property. On an average the annual toll caused by tarnadoes in the U.S.A. includes damage to property worth 100,000,000 dollars and 150 human deaths. The deadliest part of the tornadoes is the *TORNADO MISSILES* (consisting of uprooted trees, their branches, roofs of buildings etc., which are carried away by dynamic force of winds) which inflict great damage to buildings, other human structures and human lives. A tornado, for example, at Lubbock (Taxas, U.S.A.) in 1970 moved a long cylindrical fertilizer tank (3.35 m x 12.5 m in size with a weight of 11 tons) for a distance of 1.21 km from its original place.

Two great seasons of tornado outbreak in the U.S.A. tell the awful story of ravages caused by deadly tornadoes. The occurrence of tornadoes in groups involving large numbers on a specific day in the U.S.A. is called as *TORNADO OUTBREAK.* One such tornado outbreak occurred on February 19, 1884 when about 60 tornadoes struck the states of Virginia, North Carolina, South Carolina, Georgia, Alabama, Mississippi, Tennessee and Kentucky between 10 AM to 12 midnight wherein the most terrible devastation was caused by terrific wind storms ever experienced in the U.S.A. before this date. The severe tornadoes struck the rural areas and most of the cities were unaffected. Total damages caused by these tornadoes include loss of property worth 3 to 4 million US dollars, death of 800 persons, injuries to 2500 people, destruction of 10,000 buildings, homeless and destitute people numbering 10000 to 15000 and destruction of large numbers of domestic animals. The following reporting in the news paper, the Washington Post, presents a vivid picture of the sad story of 1884 outbreak of tornadoes.

"The centre of the storm struck the outskirts of Rockingham with such fury that people were unable to escape from their houses. Buildings were blown into fragments. Some bodies were found under the timbers, others were carried by the wind 150 to 300 yards. A woman was found clasping to her breast an infant scarcely a month old; both were dead. The bodies of victims were terribly bruised and cut, presenting a ghastly appearance. The force of the wind was such that two millstones were moved 100 feet. Chickens and birds were picked clean, except the feathers on their heads" (Willimington N.C.) Star in The Washington Post, 22 February 1984).

The second important outbreak of tornadoes known as the Jumbo Outbreak comprised of 148 tornadoes struck 12 central states of the U.S.A. on April 3 and 4, 1974. The city of Xenia in Ohio state was worst affected by the tornado which destroyed 5 schools within the city. Like 1884 outbreak of tornadoes, this outbreak also largely affected rural areas and avoided large cities. Total damage caused by these tornadoes in 12 US states included deaths of 300 people and injuries to 5,000 persons.

Hurricane Andrew killed 40 people and rendered 160,000 people homeless in 1992. Hurricane Fran inflicted damage to the property worth 6 billion US dollar in 1996. Hurricane Floyd which struck eastern North Carolina on September 17, 1999 killed 31 people, damaged crops worth one billion US dollar. This hurricane has been claimed as the strongest storm in the history to hit the U.S. coast (classed as category 5 and termed as most disastrous) (down to Earth, Oct. 15, 1999).

Destructions by Tropical Cyclones And Local Storms- Include loss of human lives and property in terms of destruction of buildings, transport systems, water and power supply systems, disruption of communication system, destruction of agricultural crops, domestic and wild animals, natural vegetation, private and public institutions and so on. The deadliest impact of tropical cyclones and tornadoes are on human beings. There are 6 major regions in the world which are responsible for the origin of tropical cyclones e.g., (i) West Indies, Gulf of Mexico, and Caribbean Sea; (ii) Western-North Pacific Ocean including Philippines islands, China Sea and Japanese islands; (iii) Arabian Sea and Bay of Bengal; (iv) Eastern Pacific coastal region off Mexico and Central America; (v) South Indian Ocean, off Madagascar (Malagasi) and (vi) Western South Pacific Ocean, in the region of Samoa and Fiji island and the east north coast of Australia. It may be pointed out that the occurrences of tropical cyclones are rhythmic in nature because they are restricted to certain seasons of a year. The seasons of the occurrences of tropical cyclones vary from one region to the other region. For example, hurricanes mostly affect the U.S.A. between May and November wherein the maximum frequency is recorded in the end of summer and the beginning of autumn seasons.

The following tables portray the death toll of human beings caused by tropical storms and local storms in different parts of the world.

Table 1.3 : Some Noteworthy Indian Tropical Cyclonic Disasters

Year	*Human Deaths*	*Year*	*Human Deaths*
1737	300,000	1977	55,000
1789	20,000	1998	598
1833	50,000	1998 (Gujarat)	> 1000
1839	20,000	1999 (Orissa)	> 10,000
1864	50,000		

Note : The intensity of 1990 Andhra cyclone was 25 times greater than the 1977 Andhra cyclone but human causality could be contained because of correct prediction and better warning systems but the property damage could not be stopped.

Table 1.4 : Notable Tropical Cyclonic Disasters in Bangladesh

Year	*Human Deaths*	*Year*	*Human deaths*
1822	40,000	1963	11,468
1876	100,000	1970	300,000
1879	175,000	1976	100,000
1960	5,149	1985	11,000

Table 1.5 : Typhoon Disasters in the Far East

Year	*Country*	*Human Deaths*
1881	China	300,000
1923	Japan	250,000
1960	Japan	500

Table 1.6 : Damage Caused by Natural Hazards in Japan, 1946-1970

S. No.	*Events*	*Number of events*	*Human deaths*	*Houses destroyed*
1.	Typhoon	59	13,745	576,378
2.	Extra tropical cyclone	89	8,156	65,818
3.	Earthquake	11	5,490	113,339
5.	Landslides	5	86	143
5.	Hail and thunderstorm	4	28	847
6.	Heavy snow	2	242	1,734
7.	Volcanic eruption	1	12	12

The unpredictability and ferocity of tornadoes make protection and preparedness very difficult. Nevertheless, in the period that tornado forecast and warning services have been in the operation in the U.S.A., annual average number of fatalities seem to have decreased markedly (J.E. Hobbs, 1980). According to G.P Gressman (1969) the average number of annual deaths due to tornadoes is decreasing every year as average number of deaths between 1916 and 1952 was 200 per year but this reduced to 120 between 1953-1968 because of improved warning systems. Two methods of operational detection and tracking of tornadoes are in practice in the U.S.A. viz., (i) detection and tracking of

Table 1.7 : Estimated Damages Caused by Individual Tropical Storm

November 17,1970		May 9, 1990	
Bangladesh		Andhra Coast, India	
Population affected	470,000	Population affected	300,000
Persons killed	300,000	Persons killed	598
Crop losses	63 million US $	Loss of cattle	90,000
Loss of cattle	280,000	Loss of property	100 billion Rupees
Loss of poultry	500,000	Gale wind speed	220-250 km per hour
Houses damaged	400,000		
Schools damaged	3,500		
Fishing boats destroy (in sea)	9,000		
Fishing boats destroyed (inland water)	90,000		

tornadoes by weather surveillance radar and (ii) prompt reports of visual sightings by competent observers. India has also set up more than 100 disaster warning systems and dying INSAT 1-B provided important information about the disastrous cyclones of May 9, 1990 which struck the Andhra coast. The advance monitoring and prediction of this disastrous cyclone at least a week before the final countdown and its attack on the coastal districts of Andhra Pradesh saved thousands of people from sure death trap. People had sufficient time to move to safer places and thus warning systems contained human deaths which remained below 1000 mark (official figure being 598). In the absence of warning systems and ready response of inhabitants to evacuation programme this cyclonic storm being 25 times greater in intensity than the killer cyclone of 1977 (which caused 55,000 deaths in Andhra Pradesh) might have caused unbelievable human deaths.

Gujarat coast was struck by a very powerful cyclonic storm with a velocity of more than 200 km per hour on Tuesday, June 9, 1998 and caused a surging tidal wave of 8m height which transgressed into the coastal land and caused immense loss of property and human death unknown in the cyclonic history of Gujarat. The salt workers working in the salt pans in the Runn areas of Kutch were washed away by high tidal waves. The storm was so powerful accompanied by heavy rainfall that human settlements were destroyed all the way from Surat and Amerli in Gujarat to Jalore and Jodhpur in Rajasthan. Mud-built houses were flattened, power supply was snapped, trees were uprooted and carried away as missiles, and communication and vehicular traffic were completely disrupted. The storm caused more than 1000 human deaths and economic loss worth more than 100 billion rupees (unofficial estimates put the number of death between 5,000 and 10,000). Kandla port was greatly damaged.

(C) Cumulative Atmospheric Hazards

Cumulative atmospheric hazards are those events which are caused due to cumulative effects of weather events which prolong for longer period of time ranging from a few weeks to several years depending upon the nature of weather events. For example, any hot day may not become disastrous or hazardous but when very hot and dry days prevail for a few weeks in continuation, environmental hazard in the form of heat waves occurs which affect the environment and human lives, plants and animals. The persistence of exceptionally cold conditions for several days causes severe snowfall. A dry season in a year may not be as much disastrous as continued dry seasons for several years. The perception and concept of drought vary from place to place and from one group of people to other group based on profession and occupation. In fact, drought occurs when there is appreciable decrease in rainfall from the average normal rainfall. Floods are still very severe environmental hazards which are related to atmospheric processes. Mississippi flood plains

(U.S.A.) and the Ganga plains (India) are frequented by severe flood hazards. It may be pointed out that floods are not always hazardous rather these are also boon because these bring rich fertile alluvial soil each time and thus increase agricultural productivity.

Floods

Flood simple means inundation of extensive land area with water for several days in continuation. Generally, floods are considered to be associated with rivers and people conceive flood as the outcome of accumulation of huge volume of water coming out of the rivers through overtopping of river banks during peak discharge period. In fact, flood is an attribute of physical environment and thus is a component of hydrological cycle of a drainage basin. It may be pointed out that flood is a natural phenomenon and is a response to rainfall but it becomes hazard when it causes colossal loss to human lives and property. It is also important to note that floods are also aggravated by human activity and thus flood hazard is both natural as well as man-induced rather man-accentuated phenomenon. Floods are very often associated with alluvial rivers draining extensive alluvial and flood plains. About 3.5 per cent of the total geographical area of the world is covered by flood plains which has about 16.5 per cent of the total population of the world. The most notorious rivers of the world in terms of devastating floods and resultant damage to natural environment (riparian decay) and loss of human lives and property are the Ganga and its major tributaries such as the Yamuna, the Ramganga, the Gomti, the Ghaghra, the Gandak, the Kosi, the Damodar etc. (northern India), the Brahmaputra (north-east India), the deltaic segments of the Mahanadi, the Krishna, the Godavari, the Tapti, the Narmada, the Luni, the Mahi etc. (all in India), the Mississippi and Missouri (U.S.A.), the Yangtze, the Yellow (China), the Irrawadi (Myanmar), the Indus (Pakistan), the Niger (Nigeria), the Po (Italy), the Euphratus and Tigris (Iraq) etc.

Causes of Floods—Since the floods of rivers are the responses of both natural and anthropogenic factors, the causes of floods of the alluvial rivers become highly complex and their relative importance varies from place to place. Among the natural factors which cause river floods important are prolonged high intensity rainfall; meandering courses of the rivers; extensive flood plains; break in slope in the long profiles of the rivers i.e. sudden change in channel gradient at the intervening zones of the foothill slope of the mountains and upper end of the plains; blocking of free flow of the rivers because of enormous debris provided by landslides and due to volcanic eruptions; nature of river valleys and channels etc. Anthropogenic activities such as building activity and eventual urbanization, channel manipulation through diversion of its (of the river) course, construction of bridges, barrages and reservoirs, agricultural practices, deforestation, land-use changes etc., by man invite several hazards in the river system viz., disastrous floods, landslides and slumping along the banks, massive erosion along the river banks causing large-scale riparian decay, shifting of channels and even of the river courses, silting of beds, deposition of sands, silts and clays in the flood plains etc., which pose a serious threat to human society and necessitate river regulation and flood control (Savindra Singh, 1983). The following causes may be held responsible for devastating floods of alluvial rivers. It may be pointed out that these factors should never be considered separately because it is the cumulative effects of several factors which ultimately cause severe floods.

(1) Heavy rainfall for long period in continuation is the root cause of river floods because immense volume of water either through high intensity rainfall or large-scale snow-melt is the prerequisite condition for river floods. Heavy rainfall in the upper catchments areas of the concerned river causes sudden increase in the volume of downstream water. This causes overtopping of river bank by enormous volume of water and consequent inundation and flooding of flood plain areas. It may be pointed out that the occasional heavy rainfall resulting from

strong rainstorms can cause severe flood only in those region which are characterized by seasonal regime of rainfall or say seasonality of rainfall such as the regions of monsoon climate (rainfall during four wet summer months e.g., June to September), Savanna climate (rainfall during wet summer months), Mediterranean climate (rainfall during wet winter months) etc., because of the fact that the rivers maintain very low flow and low discharge of water during most part of the year and hence sudden torrential rainfall causes sudden increase in the volume of water which cannot be disposed off by the rivers immediately and thus the river banks are overtopped by the swelling water and instantaneous floods are caused.

The unprecedented flood of the Lower Damodar river in West Bengal due to torrential cyclonic rainfall of September 26-29, 1978 explains the impact of high intensity rainfall as a potent causative factor of floods. The severe cyclonic storm yielded heavy rainfall totaling 600 mm between September 26-29, 1978 in the upper catchments of the Damodar river (falling in Bihar, India) and 500 mm in its lower catchments (falling in West Bengal) thus giving an average amount of 550 mm within a 3-day period (September 27-29, 1978). It may be pointed out that the Damodar river is a controlled river through a series of dams and reservoirs on the main river and its tributaries such as Panchet dam, Mainthan dam, Konal dam, Tilaiya dam etc., under the scheme of Damodar Valley Corporation (D.V.C.). The combined outflow of water from Maithan and Panchet dams was 16,000 cusecs (cubic feet per second) on September 23, 1978 and 10,000 cusecs on September 26, (upto the 6th hour), 1978 just before the outbreak of torrential rainfall from strong cyclonic storm centered in the upper catchments of the Damodar river. The torrential incessant rainfall resulted into enormous surface runoff which immediately reached the master stream and thereafter the reservoirs constructed behind the banks on the Damodar and its tributaries. Rapid pouring of enormous volume of water into the reservoirs caused quick rise in the level of reservoir's water and hence the discharge of outflow from the dams downstream had to be increased. Thus the outflow of water increased from 10,000 cusecs to 100,000 cusecs in the 24th hour of September 26 in response to the beginning of torrential rainfall in the upper catchments area. The discharge of outflow was noted on the next consecutive days as 160,000 cusecs on the 24th hour of September 27, 1978, 161,900 cusecs on the 3rd hour of September 28, 100,000 cusecs on September 29 and 60,000 cusecs on September 30, 1978.

Heavy rainfall also in the lower catchment having alluvial plains of West Bengal amounting to 500 mm within 3-day period and high discharge of water coming from upstream segment of the Damodar further augmented the discharge which was recorded as 379,800 cusecs on the 12th hour of September 27, 1978. This high discharge of water could not be accommodated in the valley of the Damodar in its lower reaches and hence devastating flood was generated which destroyed agricultural crops, caused heavy loss of human lives and property. High intensity rainfall giving average annual amount of 2500 mm in the plain area and 5000 mm in the hilly sector in Assam (India) causes frequent floods of high magnitude through the Brahamputra river almost every year. Heavy rainfall in the Himalayas and in the plains causes disastrous floods in the Himalayan rivers draining through the North India Plains or Ganga plains.

Increased surface runoff also accelerates the rate of soil erosion and thus increases the sediment load of the rivers. Increased sediment load causes pollution of river beds and filling of the valleys. This process results into gradual rise in the river beds and decrease in the cross sectional areas of the valleys and hence reduction in the river beds and decrease in the cross sectional areas of the valleys and hence reduction in the water accommodating capacity of the river valleys. All these chain effects of deforestation and related increased surface runoff, increased soil erosion and decreased cross sectional areas of the valley not only cause floods but also increase the magnitude and dimension of floods. Large-scale deforestation in the Himalayas for the last one hundred years or so has resulted into phenomenal increase in the frequency, magnitude and dimension of floods in those rivers which have their source catchments in the Himalayas but extensive drainage areas in the alluvial Ganga plains such as the Ganga and its tributaries like the Yamuna, the Ramganga, the Gomti, the Ghaghra, the Gandak, The *Burhi* Gandak, the Kosi etc. The extent of damages caused by swollen alluvial rivers and recurrent floods in the states of Uttar Pradesh, Bihar and West Bengal (India) is increasing every year, (5) Increasing urbanization also helps in increasing the surface runoff and therefore dimension and magnitudes of floods because extension in the pucca ground cover through the construction of building, courtyards, roads, pavements etc., reduces infiltration of rainwater significantly and increases surface runoff considerably which increases the volume and discharge of storm drains of urban areas. Thus the rainwater resulting from torrential rainfall is quickly disposed off through the city storm drains to nearby streams and thus the volume of river water is increased causing floods. Besides, obstructing of river flow due to pouring of wastes and garbage from the nearby urban centres, gradual encroachment of human settlements towards the channels and low lying areas, filling of 'nallas' (natural urban drains), construction of new roads and bridges etc., are also significant factors, related to urbanization, of floods which not only degrade the physical environment of the rivers and surrounding terrains but the recession of deluge also causes accumulation of human refuse, sewage materials, silts etc., bringing the epidemics and thus degrading the human environments in most of the reverie cities of alluvial regions of the developing countries in general and India in particular (Kanpur, Allahabad, Varanasi etc., located along the mighty Ganga river are burning examples of degradation of environment caused by recurrent floods of the Ganga river at frequent intervals).

In India valley-side slopes of alluvial rivers are ploughed down to the channel transverse to the channel or say transverse to the contours (in order to dry out the moisture accumulated due to alleviation during floods) during rabi season (winter cropping season) and the farms are never irrigated. After the crops are harvested, the ploughed fields are baked hot in the scorching sunlight of summer months with the result loose soils become extremely dry. These dried soils are soaked with water during first summer showers and are slumped into the river bed by overland flow. This slumping of moistened soils results in the gradual silting of river bed. On the other hand, the cultivation of valley-side slopes reduces the gradient of river banks. These two processes flatten the valley and thus reduces the water accommodating capacity of the river valley with the result the river takes very little time in attaining its bank full capacity and afterward water spreads over the valley sides, inundates the low lying flood plains and helps in aggravating the flood situation.

Blocking of natural flow of the rivers by landslides caused by earthquakes, other natural factors and anthropogenic factors and clearance of such blockades causes sudden severe flash floods in the downstream section of the rivers. Similarly, breaches in the dams constructed across the river also cause devastating floods in the downstream segments.

Flood Hazards in the U.S.A. and India- Most of the countries of the world suffer from river floods in one way or the other but it would be out of place to discuss the floods of each country here. The flood hazards, therefore, of the most developed country i.e., the U.S.A. and one of the leading developing countries i.e., India are briefly discussed below.

The Mississippi and the Missouri rivers are most notorious rivers of the U.S.A. as regards flood havocs caused by them at regular intervals. The U.S. rivers which are known for severe floods and carry more than 300,000 cusecs (cubic feet per second) of water discharge during peak flood periods include Escambia and Tennessee rivers (alabama state), Colorado river (Arizona), White, Red, Arkansas and Mississippi rivers (Arkansas), Eel and Kalmath rivers (California), Savannah river (Georgia), Wabash river (Indiana), Neosho and Kansas rivers (Kansas), Ohio river (Kentucky), Atchafalaya river (tributary of Mississippi, Louisiana), Potomac river (Maryland), Missouri river (Missouri state), Delaware river (New Jersey), Miami river (Ohio), Arkansas river (Oklahoma), Willamette and Columbia rivers (Oregon), Tennessee river (Tennessee), W. Nueces, Llano, Little and Pecos Rivers (Taxas), Columbia river (Washington state), Potomac and Ohio rivers (West Virginia).

Mississippi, considered as vengeful monster as regards the flood havocs caused by it, draws its waters from a vast area spreading over 30 states of the country and thus its entire drainage basin accounts for 40 per cent of the total geographical area of the conterminous U.S.A. The river adopts a highly meandering course in the extensive flood plains. The magnitude of meandering of the Mississippi may be gauged from the fact that the straight air distance between Cairo (the confluence point of the Mississippi and Ohio rivers) and its mouth in the Gulf of Mexico is 960 kilometres (600 miles) whereas the actual distance covered by the Mississippi is 2720 kilometres (1700 miles) and average channel gradient is about 3 cm per kilometre. Thus the meandering course and extremely low channel gradient and of course torrential rainfall through hurricanes and tornadoes in its extensive catchment area give the notorious character to the Mississippi river as 'both the sinuous course and low gradient of the Mississippi river so conspire to delay the passage of floods down its path that on occasion the river tops its banks and spreads in a broad sheet (off water) across the floodplain to inundate back-swamps in a belt several miles wide (A.N. Strahler and A.H. Strahler, 1976).

In March 1927, the Mississippi river rose to the highest flood crest on record. Inundation affected 18 million acres of land; thousands of families had to be evacuated from their homes. Deaths attributed to the flood numbered 313 persons; the damage in 1927 was $ 300 million (A.N. Strahler and A.H. Strahler, 1976). Missouri, Tennessee (the tributary of Ohio), Ohio, Arkansas, etc., contributed much of flood water to the

Table 1.8 : Selected Peak Discharge of Major Rivers of the U.S.A. during Floods

River	*Location*	*Drainage area (sq. miles)*	*Date*	*Flood Peak (cubic feet per second, cusescs)*	*Runoff Factor (Cusecs/ sq. mile)*
Tennessee	Savannah (Tennessee)	33,140	21.5.1897	450,000	13.6
W. Nueces	Kickapoo Springs (Taxas)	402	14.6.1935	580,000	1440.0
W. Nueces	Cline (Taxas)	880	14.6.1935	536,000	609
Nueces	Uvalde (Taxas)	1,930	14.6.1935	616,000	319
Llano	Castell (Taxas)	3,747	14.6.1935	388,000	104
Little	Cameron (Taxas)	7,000	10.9.1921	647,000	92.4
Pecos	Comstock (Taxas)	35,293	28.6.1954	948,000	26.9
Columbia	Washington	5,97,000	June, 1894	680,000	11.4
Potomac	Hancock (West Virginia)	4,073	18.3.1936	340,000	83.4
Ohio	Parkersburg (West Virginia)	35,600	29.3.1913	593,000	16.7
Tennessee	Florence (Alabama)	30,810	19.3.1897	444,000	14.4
Colorado	Lees Ferry (Arizona)	107,900	7.7.1884	300,000	2.78
Colorado	Yuma (Arizona)	242,900	22.6.1916	250,000	1.03
Mississippi	Arkansas City (Arkansas)	1,30,700	20.4.1927	2,472,000	2.19

Eel	Scotia (California)	3,113	22.12.1955	541,000	174
Klamath	Klamath (California)	12,100	22.12.1955	425,000	35.1
Savannah	Augusta (Georgia)	7,508	1976	300,000	47.9
Wabash	Mt. Carmel (Indiana)	28,600	30.3.1913	428,000	15
Neosho	Iola (Kansas)	3,818	13.7.1951	436,000	14

Mississippi floods and therefore extensive control measures have been adopted to tame Missouri, Mississippi, Arkansas and Tennessee rivers etc.

The heavy torrential rainfall accompanied by hurricanes is the major cause of flood hazards in the U.S.A. The flood hazards caused by hurricane Agnes in June 1972 in the south-eastern and eastern states of the U.S.A. very much tell the impact of atmospheric disturbances on the creation of devastating floods. The strong storm originating in the south-east of Florida struck the main land on June 19, 1972 and moved northward through the eastern coastal states of the U.S.A. to reach New Jersey on June 22, 1972. After remaining stationary from June 22 to 25 over north-eastern states (New Jersey, Pennsylvania) it moved eastward to dissipate after June 27 in the north Atlantic Ocean. This hurricane yielded rainfall between 150 mm to 230 mm in the southern states, 350 mm to 450 mm in the states of Pennsylvania and New York. This heavy amount of rainfall within a day or two caused severe floods in most of the Atlantic-bound rivers. For examples, Susquehanna river recorded its water level 4.87 m above its flood stage and Ohio river (to meet the Mississippi in the south-west) at Pittsburgh reached 3.35 m above flood stage. The worst affected rivers were Susquehanna, Juniata, and Schuylkill. The hurricane and flood disasters did the following damage in the state of Pennsylvania alone.

Floods in India—Most of the flood-prone and flood affected areas of the country are located in the northern parts mainly in the Ganga plains of the states of Uttar Pradesh, Bihar and West Bengal. The flood hazards and disasters in Uttar Pradesh, Bihar and Andhra Pradesh combined together account for 62 per cent of the total damages done by floods in the country. Table 1·9 presents the state-wise damages caused by flood hazards in India.

Table 1.9 : State-wise Share of Damages done by Floods (In percentage) (Average of 1971-78)

States	*Share of damages (in percentages)*	*States*	*Share of damages (in percentage)*
Bihar	23.9	Rajasthan	4.5
Uttar Pradesh	23.8	Tamil Nadu	3.8
Andhra Pradesh	15.4	Haryana	3.2
West Bengal	7.0	Assam	2.1
Gujarat	5.7	Punjab	1.4
Orissa	4.5	Madhya Pradesh	1.3

It may be pointed out that there is constant increase in the frequency intensity spatial coverage (dimensions) and magnitude of damages of floods in India every year because of a bunch of causative factors such as rapid rate of deforestation in the source catchments of major rivers and their tributaries and consequent accelerated rate of soil erosion, increase in sediment load of rivers, situation and rise of river beds and marked reduction in the water accommodating capacity of the river valleys; increasing urbanization, mushroom growth of settlements in the floodplains and even in the flattened (due to alleviation) valleys; encroachment of agricultural practices upon the valley sides and even down to the channels; construction of bridges, embankments and dikes etc.

During recent years both the frequency and intensity of floods have increased significantly. For example, compared to 1950-65, the average loss from floods got doubled in 1966-67 and went upto 3 times in 1971-75 and 5 times in 1976-78 showing a constant upward trend. According to another estimate, the loss caused by floods within two years (1976-78) remained more than 5 times as compared to earlier period of twelve years...... As National commission on Floods reports, the country suffers a damage of Rs 1000 crores every year on this account and the figure is rising steadily. What is more, the total area subject to flooding has doubled from 20 million ha (hectare) in 1971 to 40 million ha in 1981 (J. Singh and D.N. Singh, 1988). Table 1·10 depicts the damages done by flood hazards in India during 20-year period (1953-75).

Table 1.10 : Magnitude of Flood Damages in India

Details of Damages	*Average during 1953-1975*	*Annual Maximum Damages*
Areas affected by floods	7.4 million hectares	1.372 million hectares
Cropped areas affected	3.1 million ha	7.6 million ha
Number of houses damaged	8,00,000	23,10,000
Number of cattle lost	50,331	270,000
Number of persons died	742	3,498
Total direct losses	Rs 2104 million	Rs 8,850 million

Three Examples of recurrent severe floods of reverie urban centres viz., Lucknow and Jaunpur on Gomti river (Uttar Pradesh) and Allahabad located at the sacred confluence of two mighty rivers of India viz., the Ganga and the Yamuna tell the sad story of hazardous impacts of river floods on natural and human environment.

(*i*) "Lucknow, the capital city of the state of Uttar Pradesh, faces the ravages of floods of the Gomti river a significant tributary of the Ganga of and on. The catchment area of the Gomti at Lucknow is 8826.68 square kilometres. The flood water was naturally accommodated in the low-lying areas on both sides of the main channel before the construction of the Town Protection Embankments and extensive encroachment of human settlements but the appearance of these activities has aggravated the dimension of flood because of marked reduction in the water accommodating capacity of the channel. A record of floods from 1923 to this date (1983) reveals the varying dimensions of floods peaks and duration. Prior to the highest floods recorded so far in 1960 when the flood level at Gaughat Gauge stood at 113.2 m and the corresponding discharge was estimated as 150,000 cusecs (cubic feet per second), the city experienced a disastrous flood in 1923 when flood level touched 112.32 m at Gaughat with the estimated flood discharge of 75,000 cusecs and the low-lying areas were completely inundated. Then followed the most disastrous flood of 1960 in the living memory surpassing all the previous records of flood levels as referred to above due to sudden and heavy outburst of rainstorms in the catchments area of the Gomti river..... The Buttlerganj area which was protected by the construction of marginal embankment after 1923 flood, was badly affected as water spilled through two breaches allowing about 30,000 to 40,000 cusecs of water in the low-lying areas".

The limited waterway to pass a flood discharge of 150,000 cusecs (during 1960 flood), obstruction by eight bridges, indiscriminate encroachment in the river valley by building houses, ghats (bathing area) and other masonry structures reduced the discharge of water resulting into unprecedented disaster of flood in 1960. The year of 1971 came with gloom and despair to the inhabitants of flood-prone localities of Lucknow as the second highest flood peak of 112.5 m with estimated discharge of 107.000 cusecs crossed the danger level at Gaughat fixed at 111.0 m. The river after maintaining a silence for nine years since 1971 came again with a rigorous flood fury in 1980 when gushing water inundated several low-lying localities of the city".

(*ii*) Jaunpur City, located in the meander loop of Gomti river ...... about 60 km upstream from its confluence with the Ganga river, 261 km downstream and S.W. of Lucknow city, 58 km N.W. of Varanasi, and 90 km N.E. of Allahabad city " is very often affected by flood havocs of high magnitude. The records of floods in the past show the occurrences of high floods in 1774, 1794, 1830, 1871, 1894, 1903, 1915, 1922, 1936, 1949, 1955, 1960, 1971 and 1980. The danger level has been fixed at 74.66 m at the gauge station one km upstream of Shahi Bridge (now in bad shape). During the decade 1970-1980 flood levels crossed the danger level four times viz., in 1970 (highest flood level 75.96 m), 1971 (77.736 m), 1976 (75.33 m) and 1980 (77.25 m). The 1971 flood level surpassed all the previous records since 1871 (when all time peak of 80.4 m was reached) and inflicted a damage of Rs. 80,53,000 as the low-lying localities on the riversides and the southern part of the city were submerged about a storeydeep under water and Wallandgang (the main market area) became the main thoroughfare of the river as turbulent current of 5 m depth with a velocity of 15 to 18 km per hour swept the main Wallandgang crossing and the Shahi Bridge (Reduced level of road, 75.76 m AMSL) was under 2 m high water and thousands of people were evacuated. The level of 1980 flood (77.25 m) was though lower than 1971 flood level (77.736 m) but it surpassed all previous records of duration, dimension and horizontal extent of the flood water as 2/3rd part of the city reeled under water for about 60 days in stretch when the Gomti crossed the danger level on July 28, 1980 and a sign of relief was seen only after 10th as September, 1980 but the clearance of water took another 15 days ..... The flood inflicted a colossal loss to human life and property by swallowing 13 human lives damaging 7500 houses and incurring a property loss of Rs 25 million" (Savindra Singh, 1983, pp.) .

(*iii*) Allahabad City, located at the confluence of two mighty rivers of India, the Ganga and the Yamuna, is adversely affected by floods at regular intervals. "It is evident from table that both the rivers crossed the medium flood levels of 82 m (except the Ganga in 1981) from 1971 to 1983 which means that there is perpetual problem of recurrent medium flood in the low-lying areas on the outskirts of the city. The Ganga and the Yamuna waters crossed the danger flood levels (84.75 m) 5 times within a span of 13 years (1971-1983, table 17.19). The recurrence interval of very serious flood crossing the flood level of 88 m and maximum discharge of more than 50,000 cusecs (m^3/sec) (the Ganga) and 47,000 m^3/sec (the Yamuna) is 11 and 10 years for these two rivers respectively" (S.S. Ojha, Savindra Singh and R.C. Tiwari, 1989).

Flood Control Measures- Flood control measures include a series of steps to tame the menacing rivers such as (A) to delay the return of runoff resulting form torrential rainfall to the rivers; (B) to hasten the discharge of water; (C) to reduce the volume of water; (D) to divert the flow of water; (E) to reduce the impact of floods and above all (F) to forewarn the occurrence of floods.

It may be pointed out that the floods are natural phenomena and one cannot entirely get rid off them but their impacts can be minimized by man's technological skill, better warning systems and positive human response to flood warnings and various control measures adopted by the governments.

(A) The first and foremost step to control floods is to look into their basic cause which is perhaps the high intensity rainfall and resultant surface runoff. Man cannot stop high intensity rainfall and there is no need at all to interfere with natural processes. What man can do is to delay the return of surface run of resulting from the high intensity rainfall to the rivers. This can be achieved by large-scale reforestation and aforestation in the hilly source catchment areas of those rivers which are notorious for their recurrent disastrous floods. The thick vegetal covers mostly of dense forests help in this regard in a number of ways viz., (i) forests delay the return of rainwater to the rivers because these intercepts the falling raindrops and leaf litters and herbaceous ground covers hold waters. (ii) These encourage more infiltration of rainwater and therefore reduce, though marginally amount of surface runoff. (iii) These significantly reduce soil erosion and hence reduce sediment load of the rivers. (iv) Marked reduction in soil erosion and sediment load discourages salutation and hence reduction in the water accommodating capacity of the rivers etc. It is, therefore, apparent that making the hills having the sources of flood producing rivers green through large-scale tree plantation can effectively reduce the frequency and dimension of floods.

(B) It has already been mentioned that too much bends and meander loops in the highly sinuous and meandering rivers retard the quick disposal of water. It is, therefore, advisable to straighten the sinuous and meandering courses of the rivers at some places (where meanders and loops have become extremely sharpened) by performing artificial cutoffs of individual bends or a series of bends so that the flood discharge may move downstream more rapidly and the water may be disposed off by the rivers quickly. Such devices are required to train the alluvial rivers because these rivers (like all of the alluvial rivers of the Ganga plains e.g., the Ganga, the Ramganga, the Tapti, the Gomti, the Gandak, the Kosi etc.) develop highly meandering courses due to alluvial filled flat terrain. There are two main difficulties in the implementation of these control measures e.g., (i) the device requires huge money which may not be easily forthcoming in the developing countries and (ii) meandering is a natural process of alluvial rivers, if meanders are removed at some places, the river may develop meanders at other places. The lower Mississippi river near Greeville (U.S.A.) has been shortened in its length from 530 km to 185 km between 1933 and 1936 to reduce flood crests. Similarly, the Missouri river (U.S.A.) has been shortened in its length by 52 km between Sioux City and its confluence with the Mississippi in 1960 for flood control and navigation improvement.

(C) The volume of water during flood stage of a river may be reduced through a series of engineering devices such as construction of flood-control storage reservoirs. Such storage reservoirs impound enormous volume of water during flood period and thus these help in two ways e.g., firstly, these storage reservoirs reduce the volume of water of the rivers and secondly, these provide water for irrigation purposes. If the reservoirs are succeeded by huge dams, they also help in the generation of hydroelectricity.

Such flood-control reservoirs were constructed on Miami river in the state of Ohio (U.S.A.) as early as in 1913. A series of storage reservoirs were completed by 1921 and thus the scheme of the construction of storage reservoirs as effective flood-control measure became very popular in the U.S.A. The Tennessee basin of the U.S.A. was considered to be held till 1933 because of perpetual water logging, recurrent floods, very high incidence of malaria, typhoid and tuberculosis, accelerated rate of soil erosion and increase in the infertility of the soils and wasteland. But the construction of a series of dams and reservoirs under the scheme of Tennessee Valley Authority (T.V.A.) since 1933 has not only controlled the recurrent floods and tamed the made Tennessee river but also has entirely changed the social and economic picture of the basin to such an extent that the basin once considered as 'hell and curse' is now considered as heaven.

The success of TVA attracted more countries to launch multi-purpose rivers projects for watershed management. The scheme was also implemented in India to check floods and for other purposes. The Damodar Valley Corporation (DVC), a multi-purpose river project, was launched on the line of TVA wherein four major dams and reservoirs have been constructed on the Damodar river and its tributaries such as the Barakar and the Konar rivers for water storage and flood moderation in the lower reaches of the Damodar river. Besides flood control, the DVC also generates hydroelectricity and provides water for irrigational purposes. The four dams namely Konar, Maithan, Panchet Hill and Tilaiya have a flood storage of 1603 million cubic metres and have been in operation since 1958 and have helped considerably in the moderation of floods in the Lower Damodar Region' (K.L. Rao, 1975). Similarly, the construction of Ukai Dam and Reservoir on the Tapi (Tapti) river has almost saved the lower reaches of the river and the town of Surat from the disaster of flood hazards. Many more examples may be cited to demonstrate the positive effects of storage reservoirs on flood control.

(D) Flood- diversion systems imply diversion of flood water

in low-lying areas, depressions or artificially constructed channels bordered by artificial dykes so that the flood crests may be reduced and the flood magnitude may be decreased. For example, Ghaggar Diversion Schemes divert the water discharge of about 340 cusecs (cubic metres per second) before entering Rajasthan (India) into the depressions and in the areas between the sand dunes during flood period so that discharge of water in the main river (the Ghaggar) during flood stage may be kept within the safe limits.

(E) Embankments, dikes and flood walls are used to confine the flood water within valley or say within a narrow channel. These engineering works include the building of artificial leaves of earthen materials, stones or even concrete walls. Artificial bunds (levees) of mostly earthen materials have been constructed to protect many of the riverside cities and towns in the Ganga plains (such as Delhi, Allahabad, Lucknow etc.). Construction of dikes or artificial levees was practiced long ago in China, India etc., but there were several cases of breaches of earthen dikes and consequent more disastrous floods than natural floods. For example dike failures in great flood on the Hwang Ho River (now Yellow River) in China in 1887 brought inundation to an area of 50,000 sq miles (130,000 sq km) and death by drowning to approximately one million persons' (A.N. Strahler and A.H. Strahler, 1976). Besides protection to the towns and cities from floods by construction dikes and other engineering structures such as revetments, artificial levees or earthen dikes are also constructed on either side of the river for longer distances to protect the floodplains from floods. For example, Kosi flood Embankments running for 246 km are being used to check the westward shifting of the Kosi river (in Bihar, India) and to protect the fertile floodplains from recurrent floods and deposition of sands and coarse silts which used to render vast tracts of fertile lands unfit for cultivation. It may be pointed out that the Kosi river before the construction of flood embankments had shifted its course westwards by about 112 km. The 246 km long embankments on either side of the Kosi river have been kept wide apart about 12 to 16 km so that broad areas confined between the artificial walls (embankments/dikes) may serve as silt trap.

Bagmati Flood Control Embankments running for a distance of 241 km and 290 km long embankments along the Mahananda river under Mahananda Embankment Scheme protect about 57,000 hectares and 160,000 hectares of floodplains respectively.

Stone spurs are also used to protect the towns, cities and other important places from severe erosion during and after the floods. Under the scheme of Dibrugarh Town Protection Works stone spurs, semi-permeable spurs, pile spurs, revetments and protective dikes of about 10 km length have been constructed to protect the town from floods and erosion by the Brahmaputra river. The Jalpaiguri Town Protection Works (India) include the construction of 16 km long embankments and the shifting of existing outfall of the Karala river into the Teesta river near Jalpaiguri by 6 km downstream.

(F) Flood Control Organisation and Flood Forecasting and Warning System in India- The Constitution of Central Flood Control Board in 1954 and the establishment of the State Flood Control Boards at state level have proved beneficial in adopting several flood control measures. The flood forecasting and warning system was started in India in 1959 to monitor the flood situation in the capital city of Delhi. Since then a network of flood forecasting and warning systems has been spread over the country to monitor the flood conditions of major river basins of the country. Thus the flood forecasting centres set up in various parts of India help in the forecasting of floods in the Ganga and its tributaries (e.g. Tapti, Gomti, Ghaghra, Yamuna, Burhi Gandak, Kosi, etc.), Brahmaputra and its tributaries (i.e., Pagladiya and Burhi Dehing, Barak, Teesta), Subarnarekha, Damodar, Brahmani, Baitarni, Tapi, Narmada, Sahibi, Godavari, Ajoy, Betwa and other flood prone rivers. The flood forecasting centres collect data of rainfall and discharge rate, gauge level or flood level from various data recording centres in the jurisdiction of each flood forecasting centre and thus warn the inhabitants of particular river basin about the possible danger of floods much in advance.

Droughts

Droughts are more deadly natural environmental hazards because these are directly related to one of the three basic requirements of any form of life (such as water, air and food) that is water and are indirectly related to food because crops and other plants and animals exclusively depend upon water. Droughts resulting from accumulative effects of water scarcity cause extensive and enormous damage to agriculture and natural vegetation and therefore cause famine and starvation of human and animal population of the regions concerned. The meaning and definition of droughts are difficult propositions because there are much variations in the viewpoints and perception of droughts from one region to another and from one group of people to another. Most people are reasonably well aware when a drought situation exists, but it is very difficult to find an overall acceptable definition of drought. It clearly involves a shortage of water but can really be defend only items of particular need. The most common view of drought is of rainfall deficiency but the links between rainfall and the water which becomes available to meet demand are complex. Therefore definition of drought related ontology to water needs but also to the complex set of factors involved to supply that needed through the hydrological cycle.

It may be pointed out that increased dryness for prolonged period causing drought condition is related to the amount of rainfall, its departures from normal average annual value and local demand of water for various purposes. It is not the amount of total annual rainfall which matters for drought for wet conditions rather it is the regularity and irregularity of rainfall which matters more. For example, a more persistent and reliable amount of 200 mm of annual rainfall may not be the cause of concern of the agriculturists in dry region because their agricultural activities would be adapted to this meager amount of rainfall but the receipts of only 200 mm of annual rainfall for a few years in continuation or even in a single year in those areas which receive normal annual rainfall of 500 to 800 mm may cause crop failure and hence disastrous drought condition may prevail. According to C.E. Hounam *et al.* (1975), the agriculturist or pastorals, especially in the dry regions, has assessed the nature of local rainfall and, through years of long and sometimes bitter experience, has learned to the failure of the usual raise at a particular time, since most activities using water will be geared to that which is normally available.

It is, thus, obvious that rainfall is the main parameter for the determination of droughts but rainfall values, however, have limitations as drought indicators, so many definitions and indices incorporate other parameters such as evaporation, humidity, air temperature, solar radiation, wind, soil moisture, stream flow and plant conditions (J.E. Hobbs, 1980). The following are a few drought definitions based on the parameters of precipitation.

(*i*) **C.G. Bates (1935)-** Annual precipitation is 75 per cent or less of normal precipitation and monthly precipitation is 60 per cent or less of normal monthly precipitation.

(*ii*) **BRO (British Rainfall Organization, 1936)-** *Absolute Drought* : When there are at least 15 consecutive days with less than 0.01 inch of rainfall per day. *Partial Drought* : When there are at least 29 days having mean rainfall of 0.01 inch or less. *Dry Spell* : When 15 consecutive days receive less than 0.04 inch of rainfall per day.

(*iii*) **J.C. Hoyt (1936)-** Annual and monthly rainfall less than 85 per cent of normal rainfall.

(*iv*) **V.A. Conard (1944)-** Period of 20 or more consecutive days without 0.25 inch precipitation in 24 hours (during March - September).

(*v*) **D.A. Ramdas (1950)-** When rainfall for a week is half normal or less.

(*vi*) **A.J. Henry (1960)-** 21 days or more when rainfall is 30 per cent or less of average rainfall. Extreme droughts occur when rainfall is less than 10 per cent of average rainfall for 21 days or more.

Most of the aforesaid definitions of droughts do not have any relevance in India and in many of the tropical and sub-tropical countries because here agricultural practices are associated with distinct seasonal water regime. Failure of monsoon rainfall in India and adjacent countries adversely affects 'Kharif Crops' and causes drought conditions. According to Indian Meteorological Department (IMD) drought is defined as a situation occurring in any area when the mean annual rainfall is less than 75 per cent of the normal rainfall. IMD has further classified droughts into two broad categories viz., (i) **Severe Drought** when the deficiency of rainfall exceeds 50 per cent of the normal rainfall and (ii) **Moderate Drought** when the deficiency of rainfall is between 25 per cent and 50 per cent of the normal rainfall.

Impacts of Droughts- As referred to earlier, droughts affect all types of life-form in the biosphere ecosystem because both plants and animals directly depend on water. Any shortage of water supply adversely affects them. Thus, the impacts of prolonged droughts include ecological, economic, demographic and political aspects. Prolonged drought conditions in a given region change the biotic component of the natural ecosystem because (i) some species of plants and animals perish as they cannot withstand extreme drought conditions; (ii) some animals migrate to other places and hence there is marked decrease in the population of certain animal species; (iii) some animals die of hunger and starvation; (iv) there is stiff competition for food due to scarcity created by drought among the animals which results in the elimination of weaker animals etc. The most significant ecological impact of prolonged drought is natural control of plants and animal population.

The economic impact of droughts includes economic losses mainly due to marked decrease in agricultural production, livestock yield and even industrial production because of short supply of water. Demographic impact of drought includes depopulation of region/areas and temporary migration of affected people and animals. Many of the people of Sahelian region of tropical Africa have left the region because of persistent drought conditions. There is frequent migration of people from drought affected areas of Rajasthan, Gujarat, Maharashtra and Andhra Pradesh in India. Due to prolonged severe droughts for four consecutive years (1984 to 1987) in Gujarat and Rajasthan a large number of people temporarily shifted to Uttar Pradesh and Bihar together with their cattle though most of the people sold out their cattle at much lower prices due to total dearth of fodder. Political significance of extreme drought conditions includes the change of political power due to acute shortage of food grains caused by crop failure due to droughts (e.g., Mr. Khurschev had to step down from power in the USSR because he had to purchase wheat from the western world) and increase in the dominance of the USA, Canada etc., on drought affected poor countries because they have to depend on those developed countries which have surplus food supply. Even the fate of state and central governments of India depends on the nature and mercy of monsoon rainfall. The idea of impacts of droughts on human activities may be had from the detailed discussion of a few case studies of drought affected areas as given below :

(1) **Sahel Region-** The region extending between hot and dry desert areas of the Sahara in the north and the Savanna region in the south and running from the western part of Africa through Mauretania, Senegal, Mali, Upper Volta Niger, Nigeria, Chad, Uganda and Ethiopia in the east is called Sahel region or Sub Sahara Region. The drought zone of the Sahel is a tropical grassland and is characterized by a feast-or-famine climate wherein the life of nomadic herders and grain farmers exclusively depends upon rainfall received during a short rainy season. The growth of grasses depends upon rainfall. Even the people of Sahel depends for their drinking water upon groundwater which is replenished through rainfall. Prolonged drought results in the depletion of groundwater and hence acute

scarcity of drinking water. This region is very often frequented by severe droughts which cause extensive damage to flora and fauna and humans. The recent severe drought began in 1968 and continued upto 1975. The drought became acute during 1971 and 1972 and its cumulative effects became so disastrous that it became a Human Catastrophe by 1974. The prolonged drought for 7 years in continuation resulted in the depletion of subsurface water reserve and drying of water holes (trapped water in sands and gravels of stream beds) band low wells. The nomadic herders were compelled not to sell out their cattle which could not survive due to water shortage in the beginning of the drought and thus they became refugees and collected in special camps near the cities and towns to get small packets of food grains donated by other countries of the world. Inspite of relief measures coming from all over the world thousands of people of the Sahel region died of hunger and starvation, thirst and diseases. About 5 million cattle were claimed by severe Sahel drought. About 50,000 people in Ethiopia and millions of children are suffering from malnutrition and diseases.

(2) **Australia-** Drought is very common natural phenomenon in Australia. The Australian droughts are both frequent in recurrence and widespread in spatial coverage. A few histories of droughts would certainly reveal the magnitude of Australian droughts. The worst drought started in 1895 and continued upto 1902. The adverse impacts of this prolonged drought included sharp fall in the number of sheep from 106 million sheep in 1891 to only 54 million in 1902 and 50 per cent decrease in the number of cattle (from 14 million cattle in 1891 to 7 million in 1902). Several enormous dust storms submerged many fences under thick cover of huge amount of soils and shads, the city of Melbourne was drenched (on November 21, 1902) with dust, several towns in the interior part could not see the sun on that day (November 21, 1902) because of thick layer of dust in the air, railway lines at many places were buried under thick deposits of loose soil and sands. Severe hazardous droughts again occurred during 1911-1916 and 1919-1920. Thus the three phases of severe droughts viz., (i) 1895-1903; (ii) 1911-1916 and (iii) 1919-1920

resulted in marked decrease in the agricultural and which was increased substantially after 1866. It may be pointed out that favorable rains during 1860's and 1870's led to phenomenal increase in the cropped area as the cultivated lands were extended from more favorable coastal areas to the inland marginal areas. The cropped land in the south-east Australia increased six times between 1866 and 1900 but the aforesaid three consecutive phases of severe droughts forced the farmers to retreat towards the favorable coastal areas. The recent severe droughts in Australia include two widespread dry spells at 1965-66 and 1967-68 which caused decrease in the farm gross national products by 20 per cent.

(3) The aforesaid examples of droughts are related to those areas which are already rain deficient regions and droughts are very common features but there are other areas where there is no problem of large-scale droughts. In such areas a drought causes serious problems of various sorts. The example of 1975-76 drought in U.K. reveals this fact. The twelve-month periods (from May 1, 1975 to April 30, 1976) recorded less than 60 per cent of normal annual precipitation. The dry conditions continued for further four months i.e., from May, 1, 1976 to August, 1976. This prolonged dry spell resulted into acute shortage of supply of water for domestic and industrial purposes as the reservoirs could not be filled up to their capacities. There was also substantial fall in agricultural production as wheat, barley, oats and potato productions in England and Wales fell by 22,12,12 and 13 to 40 per cent respectively. The total loss to agricultural production amounted to more than 500 million pounds. The gravity of the 1975-76 drought may be gauged from the fact that the government appointed a Drought Minister to handle the problems arising out of the drought.

(4) **India-** Since monsoon climate and associated rainfall is very much deceptive, irregular and uncertain, and hence nearly most parts of the country are affected by droughts and floods in one way or the other. For example, Rajasthan is a chronic drought-prone area but heavy rainfall during the first two weeks

of July 1990 (exceeding 500 mm a day) caused severe floods in most part of Rajasthan. The chronically drought affected areas of the country include 67 districts where drought, includes larger tracts in the states of Rajasthan, Gujarat, Haryana, Maharashtra, Karnataka, Andhra Pradesh and southern Uttar Pradesh. The severe drought-prone areas of India are divided into 3 zones viz., (*i*) Desert and semi-arid regions spread over an area of about 600,000 km^2 and form a rectangular tract which stretches from Ahmedabad to Kanpur (to form eastern and south-eastern border), from Kanpur to Jalandhar (to form north-eastern and northern boundary) and from Jalandhar to Rann of Kutch along the western international border. The region is characterized by low rainfall ranging between 350 mm and 750 mm per annum but the extreme western desert areas receive even less than 350 mm annual rainfall. This zone includes whole of Rajasthan and Gujarat, western and south-western parts of Punjab, most of Haryana, south-western part of Uttar Pradesh narrow strip along the western and north-western border of Madhya Pradesh. There is little impact of droughts in Punjab and Haryana because sufficient irrigational facilities are available but the area having no irrigational facilities are the worst drought affected and famine areas of the country.

(*ii*) The second chronic drought-prone zone forms a rectangular tract which spreads over the rains deficient areas of the Western Ghats. In fact, this zone is situated to the east of the Western Ghats and extends in a width of 300 km. It includes south-western Andhra Pradesh, eastern Karnataka (east of Western Ghats) and south-western Maharashtra (east of Western Ghats). This region covers 370,000 km^2 of area and is characterized by highly erratic mean annual rainfall of less than 750 mm.

(*iii*) Beside the aforesaid two broad zones of severe droughts, there are some scattered pockets of droughts in the country such as Tirunelveli district located to the south of Vagai river, Coimbatore area, Palamau area of Bihar, Purulia district of West Bengal, Kalahandi region of Orissa etc. The scattered pockets of drought-prone areas cover about 100,000 km^2 of area.

The ministry of Agriculture has identified drought affected area in the country on the basis of rainfall distribution, frequency of occurrence of drought and percentage of irrigation. On the other hand the Irrigation Commission has demarcated drought-prone areas on the basis of rainfall and irrigation in the region concerned. Thus, according to the Irrigation Commission, those areas are drought affected areas which have less than 1000 mm of mean annual rainfall, 20 per cent or more of the year do not receive even 75 per cent of this annual amount of rainfall and where irrigated areas are less than 20 per cent of the cropped areas.

Drought Control Measures-Unlike floods, forewarning is not possible in the case of droughts, through computer-based study of numerous climatic and meteorological parameters may provide some idea about the nature and pattern of precipitation in the ensuing year. Even the amount of air moisture and precipitation may be increased through anthropogenic activities such as forestation. The usual practice prevalent in most of the country to combat droughts is to provide relief measures to drought affected people. Such measures are also necessary because these provide immediate relief to the affected people. Besides, there should be long-term measures to ameliorate the severity of droughts. Such measures include afforested to increase the content of air moisture, to increase the amount of precipitation, to increase the rate of infiltration of rain water and hence the replenishment of groundwater and rise of water table; introduction of dry farming techniques to reduce the dependence of farming on rainwater; checking of desertification or desert spread; introduction of water conservation schemes; development of horticulture and pastures; revitalization of Drought-Prone Area Programmes (DPAP); construction of reservoirs, digging of wells etc.

CHAPTER 2

Vulnerability Analysis and Mitigation-Key to Disaster Management

R. B. SINGH

Department of Geography, Delhi School of Economics, University of Delhi, Delhi – 110 007.

Introduction

Disaster management is a multi-disciplinary area, covering a wide range of monitoring, evacuation, search and rescue, relief, reconstruction and rehabilitation. It is also multi-sectoral administration; scientists, planners, volunteers and communities, all have important roles to play. These roles and activities span the pre-disaster, during and post-disaster phases. Since their activities are complementary as well as supplementary to each other's there is a critical need for co-ordination in their actions.

There has been a paradigm shift of emphasis in the last decade from disaster relief to prevention and mitigation strategies. Post occurrence treatment of disasters has proved an insufficient measure for proper protection of lives and property. There is also an emphasis on mainstreaming disaster management in everyday governance by treating it as an integral part to policy formation and implementation process. Shift of emphasis from disaster response to risk reduction has opened up areas of exploratory research in the subject of disaster management.

Disaster Vulnerability

Vulnerability refers to the susceptibility of a community to a hazard. The prevailing conditions include physical, socio-economic and political factors that adversely affect its ability to respond to hazards or disaster events (Fig. 2.1).

Vulnerability analysis seeks to predict disasters by ensuring timely preparedness on the part of people and institutions and concerned government agencies. Disaster management as a growing arena of state action raises questions related to new public management and public choice paradigms. Though civil society, typified by non-government organisations, has taken an active part in restorative and rehabilitation measures, it is the government agency that is expected to function as the prime mover besides being the *regulator* and the *facilitator*.

Disaster Mitigation

The emerging arena of disaster mitigation is becoming an integral aspect of development planning, policy formulation and implementation of particular significance in the wake of the *new public management* contention of expected roll back of the state and ascendant civil society and private corporate sector.

Traditionally, disaster management consisted primarily of reactive mechanisms. However, the past few years witnessed a gradual shift towards a more proactive, mitigation-based approach, as it was being proved time and again that reactive mechanism yielded only temporary results, at a very high cost. In this context, an exploration of the concept of 'sustainable development' inevitably ensures the recent definitions of sustainable development encompass the three dimensions of economic efficiency, social equity and environmental protection, all three of which contribute to, and are affected by natural disasters.

The relationship between disaster, hazard, vulnerability can be understood as:

Disaster Risk: Hazard x Vulnerability-Capacity

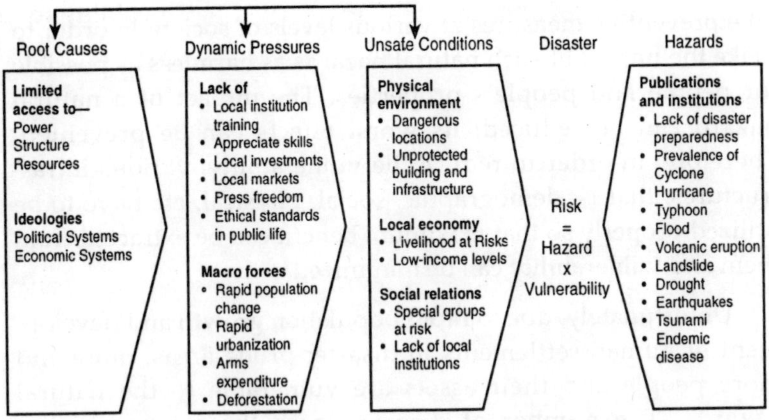

Fig. 2.1 :The model 'progression of vulnerability' with three main levels : root causes, dynamic pressure and unsafe conditions (Blaikie *et al.*, 2004)

On the other hand, disaster relief personnel have repeatedly been confronted with the same kinds of problems in a number of disaster situations. There is an increasing recognition of the fact that relief, rehabilitation and other disaster mitigation action should be coupled with interventions aimed at development. Only by overcoming poverty, developing infrastructure, inculcating awareness and spreading literacy can reduce vulnerability. In this respect, all development programmes that are committed to sustainability are relevant to disaster mitigation and prevention.

One of the many lessons learnt by victims, of various natural disasters, is that the aftermath of the disaster can be even worse than the disaster event itself. Thus, there is a need to acknowledge the necessity for preparedness towards disaster reduction. However, people are often surprised by the concept of reducing disasters. It is often asked, whether a natural disaster, such as an earthquake or a cyclone, can be reduced or prevented?

Natural occurrences such as floods, earthquakes, cyclones, etc., simply cannot be stopped from taking place; they are a part of the environment we live in. What can be done, however, is to take preventive measures at various levels of society in order to make the impact of such natural hazards as harmless as possible for people and people's properties. The impact of a natural hazard can be reduced; its worst effects can be prevented. Therefore, in order to reduce the vulnerability, various infrastructures, that is, demographic, social, physical, etc have to be utilized properly so that maximum benefit can be extracted from them and vulnerability can be minimized.

Unfortunately, due to rapid population growth and development of human settlements in disaster-prone areas, more and more people and their assets are vulnerable to the natural hazards. The number of disasters was three times higher worldwide in the past ten years than that in the 1960s. Economic losses were eight times higher, exceeding US$ 60 billion a year.

Role of Remote Sensing, GIS and GPS in Disaster Management

Satellite remote sensing is very effective in mapping disaster-prone areas particularly flood-affected areas. Microwave data can provide information on flood-inundated areas even under clouds, which is not possible with optical data. In India, microwave data from ERS-1 SAR are operationally used along with optical data from IRS-1A/1B/1C for flood management. Space technology is also being used for issuing of flood warning through collected data from data collected platforms.

Along with the development and demonstration of remote sensing based yield models for wheat and rice and a crop assessment system for wheat; mapping saline/alkaline soils of entire country on 1:250,000 scale and for selected districts on 1:50,000 scale, inventory and mapping of land-use/land-cover, using high resolution data for the whole country at 1:250,000 scale and of cultivable wastelands of specific areas at 1:50,000 scale. Under the drought monitoring and early warning project, vegetation index map, which is based on the concept that vegetation vigour is an indicator of drought, have been prepared, using NOAA-AVHRR data. The composite vegetation index maps are compared with ground parameters to establish interrelationship.

Global Positioning Systems (GPS) is another important Geospatial tool, which provides latitude, longitude and altitude of any given place on earth. GPS is based on the constellation of 24 high altitude satellites called Navigation System with Time and Ranging or NAVSTAR. The satellites are positioned in six earth centered orbital planes with four satellites in each plane. The altitude of satellite from the center of the earth is about 26,000 km. GPS makes use of the time of arrival (TOA) of the GPS signal to determine positions on earth surface. The availability of GPS has made it very easy to locate and map one of the most difficult terrains on the earth such as mountains, dense rain-forest. It also has a vital role to play in determining the extent of hazards and disasters. With the spatio-temporal analysis of GPS readings for a particular place various geological/tectonic movements can be detected and necessary warnings could be issued in case of prediction of earthquakes and disasters such as volcanic eruptions.

With the use of GIS and Remote Sensing, areas vulnerable to both natural and man-made disasters along with their varying degree of vulnerability can be established and previously made maps can be updated very easily. Such processes make planning and policy very easy for implementation. With the use of remote sensing satellites the path of cyclones can be monitored and it can provide ample time with warning for evacuation and preparedness in advance for incoming hazards.

GIS has important role to play in landslide hazard assessment because of – spatial modeling, models can be created and displayed to reflect hazards, implication of hazard in terms of risk and planning can be depicted. The maps are based on various variables for analysing landslides like slope angle, bed rock lithology, distance from faults, slope aspects, vegetation density, presence of settlements, rainfall and water, sediment type and effect of dams. One of the initial attempt was taken by the Central Road Research Institute in 1984 in which hazard zonation techniques were used to choose the most suitable alignment from the possible alternatives alignment on landslide affected stretches in Sikkim area. In case of floods, the runoff and discharge levels of the flood prone river can be monitored on the basis of the information related to physiography, altitude, rainfall, drainage, soil, vegetation, etc., that can also control the erosivity factor such as soil erosion, sediments of river, rise in river bed and ultimately floods.

These spatial information technologies i.e., Remote Sensing, GIS and GPS, will help in creating frameworks and models for creating and understanding the complex nature of disasters involving physical as well as socio-economic dimensions. In this respect the capacities and vulnerabilities analysis (CAV) can help to make the relief interventions more developmental but has been used more widely in disaster preparedness and mitigation. It's a practical and distant tool. Under the CAV framework a simple matrix is used for viewing people's vulnerability and capacities in three broad terms, interrelated areas, physical/material, social/organizational, motivational/attitudinal. The physical/material vulnerability includes land, climate, environment, health, skills and labour, housing, finance, infrastructure and technologies. To understand the physical vulnerability one has to ask what made people vulnerable: was it their economic activity, geographic location or poverty/lack of resources. The social/organizational vulnerability and capacity aspects includes formal political structure and informal systems through which people get their things done. To explore this aspect one has to ask what the social structure was before the disaster and how well it served the people when disaster struck. The motivational/Attitudinal vulnerability and capacity includes how people in society view themselves and their ability to affect their environment. Questions need to be asked here include what people's beliefs and motivations are, how disasters affect them.

Role of Communities in Disaster Mitigation

Mitigation refers to effort for reducing the actual or probable effects of a disaster on people, structures, economic and social systems and the environment. Mitigation seeks to reduce risk, that is, vulnerability to damages or losses. Mitigation focuses on the hazard that causes the disaster and attempts to minimize the adverse impacts of the hazard or communities. The reason to focus on mitigation disaster impacts include rising economic and social costs of disasters, existence of technical know-how to reduce disaster impacts and costs, and the fact that mitigation is an integral part of sustainable development.

Pre-disaster mitigation helps ensure faster recovery of a community from the economic and other impacts of disasters. Hazard reduction measures should take into account the various hazards faced by the community, including technological hazard. Potential mitigation measures should be evaluated for cost-benefit and should be consistent with the desires and priorities of the affected community, both those who will pay and those who will be benefited. Mitigation measures should protect natural and cultural resources of the community. An effective mitigation programme is based on partnerships involving the government, the private sector, and the community groups.

CHAPTER 3

Natural Hazards and Disasters: Management For Sustainable Development

PROF. B. L. TELI

Department of Geography, H. N. B Grahwal University,
Pauri -Garhwal (246 001).

Any events or accident whether caused by natural processes or by human factors are called extreme events which occur very rarely and aggravate natural environmental processes to cause hazards and disasters to human society. Tsunami, volcanic eruption, prolonged droughts, floods, atmospheric disturbances, collision of celestial bodies, etc., nuclear disaster, leakage of poisonous gases, spilling of huge quantity of crude oil in the sea and ocean, massive landslides, cyclones, cloud burst etc., hazards are those extreme events which exceed the tolerable magnitude within or beyond certain time limits, make adjustment difficult, resulting catastrophic losses of property, incomes and lives. Hazards are those processes natural or man-induced, intentional or unintentional, lead to the occurrence of extreme events whereas disasters are responsible in relation to human society and inflicts heavy damage to human property and lives. And hence it is not their frequency which makes many events hazardous or disastrous but it is the intensity, magnitude and dimensional and the quantum of damages make it hazardous and disastrous. Sometimes it is the effect of such extreme events on other natural and human processes which become disastrous.

The Natural or environmental hazards and disasters are divided into two parts – natural environmental and man-induced environmental hazards. Natural environmental hazards and disasters are sub-divided in two subcategories viz. planetary natural environmental and extra-terrestrial hazards. The terrestrial natural hazards are caused by the endogenetic forces originating deep within the earth and atmospheric, dynamic and related process originating from the atmosphere. The terrestrial hazards and disasters include volcanic eruption, seismic events, land- slides while the natural environmental hazards and disasters are caused due to extreme atmospheric processes such as tropical cyclone– hurricanes, typhoons and cyclones, tornadoes, thunderstorms, lightning, hailstorms, cloud burst and flash floods etc. And cumulative atmosphere hazards and disasters such as floods, droughts, heat waves and cold waves.

Apart from these floods, droughts, cyclones, landslides and avalanches some of the natural disasters that repeatedly and increasingly affect the world environment. The face of growth and expansion without comprehensive understanding or safety nets has brought forth a number of issues that can put man and his surroundings at a risk of perspective hazards- air accidents, boat capsizing, buildings collapse, electric fires, festival related disasters, forest fires, mine fire and flooding, oil spills, rail accidents, road accidents, serial bomb blast, under fires and village fires, the existing safeguard system is limited and risk is high. Hence a sound understanding of the vulnerability concept is must. It means the extent to which a community, structure service or geography are likely to be damaged or disrupted by the impact of particular hazards on account of their nature construction and proximity to hazardous terrain or a disaster prone area.

Disasters, man-made or natural have widespread recursion on human life, property and environment. Nature has provided abundant resources but indiscriminate and rampant growth is a threat of destruction. The relation with nature is to be balanced between men, animals and resources oil spills, forest fires or nuclear leaks can cause widespread and irreparable damage to the environment. Therefore measures for safety, maintenance and containment have to be strengthened. Global warming and extreme climates have emerged as areas rising concern.

India is experiencing massive and rapid urbanization. It is estimated that by 2025 the urban component, which was only 25.7% in 1991 will be more than 50%. High density areas with poorly built and maintained infrastructure are subjected to natural hazards, environmental degradation, fires, floods and earthquake. Urbanization dramatically increases vulnerability whereby communities are forced to squat on environmentally unstable areas such as steep hillsides prone to landslide by the side of rivers that regularly faces flood or on poor quality ground causing building collapse. The human activities are main cause of environmental degradation and disturbance to natural ecosystem all over the world.

The hilly region of India have wide variations in topography geology, soil climate, flora and fauna and various ethnic groups having different socio-cultural traditions, is a unique geographical entity of our country. All the major natural disasters hit this region causing disruption in socio-economic life of the people and bring misery to the people. Communities settled in river banks are predominantly depend on rain-fed agriculture and have a problem of flood and flood insecurity. Natural disasters primarily cyclones and accompanying cyclone surges bring miseries to the coastal communities. The damages incurred due to these disasters have grown in recent past.

The main cause is the growing population pressure in the coastal region and predicted climatic changes resulting rise in sea level. The natural occurrences of disasters cannot be stopped from taking place. But we can take preventive measure to make the impact harmless for undertaking rescue, relief and rehabilitation measures in concern state government. Since the subject of disasters management does not find mention in any of the three lists in the 7th schedule of the constitution, the rate of control government is supportive like—financial resources; warming, transport and interstate movement of foodgrains etc. It requires the multi hazards approach involving all concern agencies in the system approach. A high powered committee was constituted in August 1999 chaired by K.C. Pant. The disasters identified by high powered committee are :

1) Chemicals disasters, nuclear radiation and disasters, gaseous disasters, drugs and drinks.
2) Population bomb, unemployment, urban growth of slums, illiteracy, civil strife, commercial violence, terrorism, wars and attack.
3) Drinking water, groundwater depletion, water pollution.
4) Politics, corruption.
5) Pollution – air, water, noise and soil.
6) Food insecurity- malnutrition, hunger, chemicals products.
7) Desertification, reduction of glaciers, climatic changes.

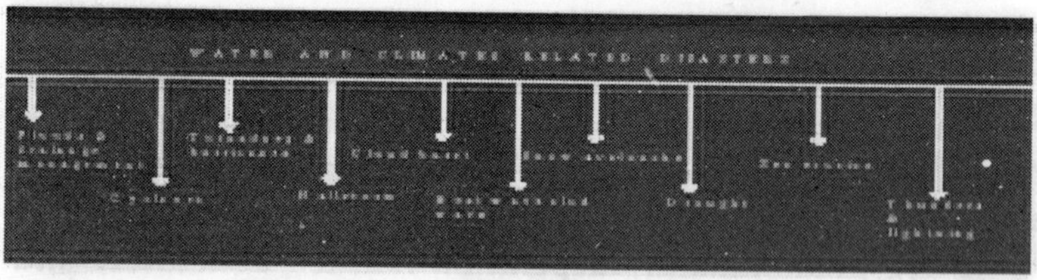

FIG. 3.1

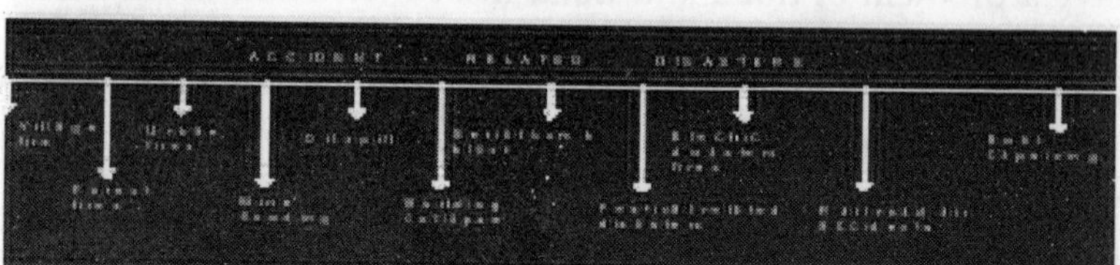

FIG. 3.2

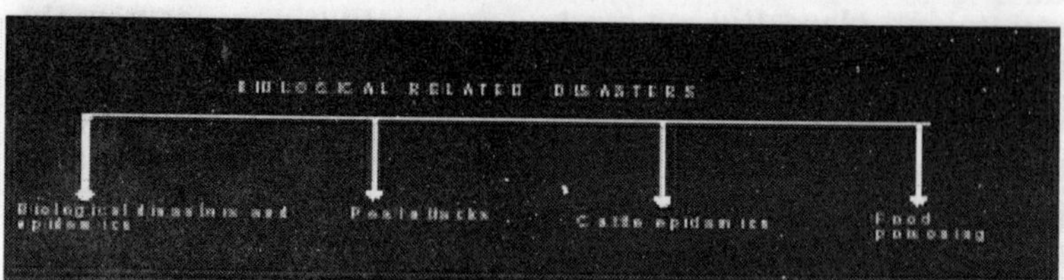

FIG. 3.3

Management

The approach towards coping with the effects of natural and man-made disasters have been post disasters management involving many problems such as–law and order, evacuation and warning, communications search and rescue, fire fighting, medical and psychiatric assistance, provision for relief and sheltering etc. After the initial trauma of occurrence of the disasters over within no time, hours or few days or weeks, the phase of reconstruction and economic, social and psychological rehabilitation is taken up by the people themselves and by the government authorities to historic memory till the next one occurs again in the same area or in some other part.

It is not possible to do away with the devastation of natural hazards completely. But the devastation from the hazards can be minimized by the presence of well functioning warning system, combine with preparedness on part of the vulnerable community. It reduces and modifies the scale of disasters. A community region or area that is prepared to face disasters, receives and understands warning of implementing hazards and has taken precautionary and mitigatery measures, will be able to cope better and resume their normal life sooner. It is therefore important to emphasis on ways and means of preventing and preparing for disasters. This protective approach is better than, waiting for history to repeat itself. There is need today, to examine the relation between environmental degradation and vulnerability to disasters and their effects on nature and man-made habitats. It also needs coordinated efforts to reduce vulnerability to disasters. Though preventive measures will not halt earthquake or cyclones but the impacts on environment can be checked.

Institutionalize a standing committee of groups of ministers – Defence, Health, Agriculture, Railways, Surface transport, Power etc., and cabinet secretary, chaired by Home minister, the chiefs of – army, air force and navy, secretaries of concern ministries. At the state level an appropriate organization should be set up to cope with incoming relief and rescue measures in disasters situation of colossal magnitudes, no time is lost in direct finding to the exact location where required. There should be knowledge pertaining to disasters and institutes engaged in the field. A national natural disasters knowledge network is proposed. It required traditional and modern knowledge to be utilized for effective disasters management. Networking of knowledge for planning is needed for research in improvement of forecasting disastrous situations.

We should not forget that aftermath of the disasters can be even worse than the disastrous event itself. Thus, there is a need to acknowledge the necessity for efforts towards disasters prevention. Natural hazards cannot be stopped but by preventive measures, we can make them harmless by reducing the worst effects towards the lives and economy of the poor and needed.

CHAPTER 4

Role of Remote Sensing and GIS Technology

RAJESH KUMAR AND GIRDHARI LAL YADAV
Lecturer, G.B. Podar College, Nawalgarh.

Introduction

Remote sensing is the acquisition of information about the biosphere by non-contact methods; usually from airplanes or satellites, in any portion of the electromagnetic spectrum. It is one of the areas of rapidly advancing technology that make it possible to deal more effectively with very large ecosystems. The exciting prospect is that remote sensing will be a logical bridge between intensive ecological research on small areas and the applications of principles thus revealed to planning and management of large political units such as townships, countries or states, or whole natural units such as watersheds, tropical rain forest, or oceans basins.

Photography from the ground or from aerial platforms is a familiar and conventional form of remote sensing that has been used extensively since the 1930s by foresters (Avery, 1966), geologists, and geographers (Avery and Richter, 1965) to inventory timber stands, to map geological structures, and to document land-use patterns. Nearly all topographic maps are now made from stereoscopic photography. The recent introduction of a laser profilometer (Remple and Parker, 1965) which measures very small differences in elevation by the time versus distance relationship of a highly focused light pulse, promises to replace expensive ground surveying for vertical control of these maps. The same technology is being used to measure distances to the moon to the nearest foot.

Distance: How Far is Remote?

As the name implies, remote sensing occurs at a distance from the object or area of interest. Interestingly, there is no clear distinction about how great this distance should be. The distance could be 1 meter, 100 meters, or >1 million meters from the object or area of interest. In fact virtually all astronomy is based on remote sensing.

Remote sensing techniques may also be used to analyze inner space. For example, an electron microscope and associated hardware may be used to obtain photographs of extremely small object on the skin, in the eye, etc. Similarly, an X-ray device is a remote sensing instrument where the skin and the muscle are equivalent to the atmosphere that must be penetrated, and interior bone or other matter is often the object of interest.

Natural Disaster Management

Mapping of affected area, severity assessment, damage estimation, monitoring and risk potential assessments of different natural disasters have been demonstrated in different parts of India. Operational monitoring of forest fire in Gir forests of Gujarat and landslide risk zonation for Tehri area has been carried out. Risk assessment for moraine dammed lakes in Himalayan regions have been demonstrated. Availability of high-resolution data from IRS 1C/D makes it feasible to assess the damage on detailed level. The technology can be used for natural disasters like :

- Floods
- Drought s
- Forest fires
- Landslides
- Earthquakes

Urban Planning and Development

Students were initially carried out for urban sprawl and growth mapping for metropolitan and smaller cities in collaboration with urban development authorities. Urban development planning for land-use suitability have been carried out for Urban Development Authorities using digital analysis and GIS tools. Use of multi-parameter weighting method down to 1:12500 scale mapping was done in Ahmedabad city :

- Mapping of urban growth and sprawl
- Land-use suitability for urban development planning
- Transportation route planning
- Utility planning and distribution planning in GIS framework
- City map updating and tourist guide maps

Watershed Development and Water Resources Development

Area specific development measures are suggested for integrated land and water resources planning based on modeling of multi-thematic inputs in GIS environment. Integrated local specific action plan are generated for sustainable development at 1:50000 and at cadastral level (1:12500) for implementation. The maps show areas for soil conservation, development of forestry, wasteland, agriculture and groundwater exploration and rainwater harvesting. Visual interpretation techniques have been developed for groundwater targeting under diverse terrain condition of India. Water harvesting sites selection, mapping of surface water resources, river migration pattern and estimation of snow-melt runoff were carried out on user request in different parts of India.

- Integrated land and water conservation and development plans for :

  (*a*) Characterization and prioritization of areas, implementation of specific analysis (*b*) Groundwater recharge and soil conservation, monitoring

(*c*) Impact analysis

- Integrated spatial database in GIS environment
- Wasteland development planning
- Groundwater targeting and sites for recharge
- Surface water resources and reservoir siltation and volume estimation
- Snow melt runoff estimation
- Glaciers: Glacier mapping and information system, disaster assessment of moraine dammed lakes

Coastal and Marine Applications

Entire coastal zone of India covering a 7500 km long coastline has been mapped on 1:250000, 1:50000 and 1:25000 scales depicting various coastal land-use, wetlands etc. The maps have been used for selection of aquaculture sites, coastal regulation, zone delineation and environment monitoring in general and for protected areas like marine national parks. Feasibility of monitoring coastal processes of currents, waves and tides, and water quality evaluation for suspended sediment and chlorophyll have been demonstrated.

Operational forecast of potential fishing zones based on SST derived from NOAA-AVHRR data and its dissemination on to fishermen through state agencies has been achieved. Site prioritization of surface water bodies for inland fisheries development has been carried out.

- Land-use mapping for coastal regulation zone (construction set – back line) upto 1:12500 scale
- Inventory of coastal wetlands, coral reefs, mangroves, seaweeds
- Site selection for brackish water aquaculture, industries, recreation, infrastructure

- Coastal erosion and sedimentation
- Monitoring and condition assessment of protected areas
- Potential marine fishing zones
- Inland fisheries development by prioritization of surface water bodies for aquaculture

Agriculture and Horticulture

Space Application Center has pioneered remote sensing based crop estimation through national projects on crop acreage and production for major crops like wheat, rice, sorghum, groundnut, cotton, and mustard in nearly 80 mha geographical area in 15 states of India. Highly diverse agricultural condition – ranging from vast monocropping systems to dry land farming and subsistence farming ensures a robust package for this challenging application. Accuracy achieved for state and district level are better than 5 and 15 per cent for production forecasts. Methodologies for crop acreage estimation for microwave data of ERS and RADARSAT satellites and for horticulture crop inventory and condition assessment have developed and demonstrated.

- Crop statistics: Single and multiple pre-harvest estimates of acreage, yield and production for major and minor crops
- Crop condition assessment: Information on comparative evaluation, yield losses, severity level
- Agricultural management: Crop water requirement for command area
- Horticultural crop assessment: Area estimation, crop / condition, site suitability analysis
- Software package for crop inventory: Capeman Software for semi-automated crop inventory

Forest Management

Visual and digital analysis techniques and GIS based methods have been developed for forest resource mapping and monitoring in collaboration with central and state forestry departments and related agencies. Modeling techniques have been applied for biodiversity and biomass assessment due to fires, encroachment, deforestation, and for grassland inventory and river valley project evaluation.

- Mapping of area, type, density of forests and deforestation and encroachment evaluation
- Forest fire assessment, zonation and monitoring
- Fuel wood estimation and biotic pressure zoning
- Biomass and tree volume modeling in plantation crops
- Area estimation of grasslands
- Forest management planning, forest stock evaluation and catchments area treatment planning
- Ecological studies on local and regional level and change detection

Environment

Studies relating to various facets of ecology and environment have been carried out using visual and digital techniques and GIS tools. Methodologies/procedures have been developed for environmental assessment and monitoring in case of mining, thermal power generation and river valley projects, and for sewage site selection for pollution abatement in polluted rivers. Maps showing India's wetlands and their comprehensive database have been prepared.

- Environment impact assessment of mining, thermal power plants, industrial development and river valley projects
- Site selection for industrial, sewage plant and tourism / resort
- Wetland mapping and inventory
- Mapping of potential hot spots and zoning of environmental hazards

Infrastructure Development Planning and Civil Engineering

Methodology for industrial site selection has been developed based on physical search as well as condition based analysis of multi-layer data. Transport route planning and utility location for public amenities and distribution planning have been used for local municipal corporation and transport agencies.

- Route and corridor planning for rail, road and highway
- Telecommunication network planning using topographic and land-use analysis
- Microhydel potential estimation by river runoff analysis
- Connectivity analysis of village and towns
- Marketing and distribution/collection center planning
- Energy Infrastructure planning
- Tourism development sites like resorts, wetlands and beaches sources (Agricultural produce, forest, minerals etc.) and infrastructure
- Sewage treatment and waste disposal sites

Engineering Geology and Mineral Exploration

Geological mapping showing structural elements and rock types has been done for four states at scales ranging from 1:1m to 1:50000 m for different state geology departments. Feasibility of locating mineralized zones and extension of existing mineral zones has been demonstrated using visual interpretation techniques.

Towards offshore oil exploration, methodology for generating prospecting geoid and gravity anomaly maps established and validated for entire Indian offshore areas using Geosat /ERS-1 altimeter data. Known oil bearing structures like Bombay High are clearly demarcated and prospective zones could be marked out for further exploration for Indian offshore area.

- Hydrocarbon prospect delineation using altimeter derived gravity anomaly and prospecting geoid maps for offshore and deep ocean areas
- Geological mapping for inland oil and mineral exploration
- General geological and geomorphological mapping in diverse terrains

Spatial Database and Information System

GIS based integrated multi-thematic resources data sets with socio-economic attributes for decision support through query and modeling have been developed for different user organizations.

- Urban information system
- District level watershed information system
- Wetland information system (Attribute)
- Glacier information system

Advantages

Remote sensing is unobtrusive if the sensor is passively recording the electromagnetic energy reflected from or emitted by the phenomenon of interest. This is a very important consideration, as passive remote sensing does not disturb the object or area of interest. Remote sensing devices are often programmed to collect data systematically, such as within a single 9*9 in frame of vertical aerial photography or a matrix (raster) of Landsat image data. This systematic data collection can remove the sampling bias introduction in some *in situ* investigations.

Under carefully controlled condition, remote sensing can provide fundamental biophysical data, including: x, y location z elevation or depth, biomass, temperature, moisture content, etc. In this sense it is much like surveying, providing fundamental data that other sciences can use when conducting scientific investigations. However unlike much of surveying the remotely sensed data may be obtained systematically over very large geographic areas rather than just single point observations.

Limitations

Remote sensing science has limitations. Perhaps the greatest limitation is that utility is often oversold. It is not a panacea that will provide all the information needed for conducting physical, biological, or social science. It simply provides some spatial, spectral, and temporal information of value. Human beings select the most appropriate sensor to collect the data, specify the resolution of the data, calibrate the sensor, select the platform that will carry the sensor, determine when the data will be collected, and specify how the data are processed. Thus, human method produced error may be introduced as the various remote sensing instrument and mission parameters are specified.

Powerful active remote sensor system, such as lasers or radars that emit their own electromagnetic radiation, can be intrusive and affect the phenomenon being investigated. Additional research is required to determine how intrusive these active sensors are.

CHAPTER 5

Major Indian Earthquakes (after 1956) and Its Impact on Indian Economy

RAVINDRA PRATAP SINGH

M.Phil., Department of Geology,
University of Delhi, Delhi-110 007.

Introduction

A tremor of the earth's surface usually triggered by the release of underground stress, this release causes movement in masses of rock and resulting shock waves, called seismic waves and this nimble process is called as "Seismic Activity".

In common words we can say, 'Sudden shaking of the ground caused by a disturbance deeper within the crust of the earth is an Earthquake or Seismic Activity.'

At the Earth's surface, earthquakes may manifest themselves by a shaking or displacement of the ground and sometimes cause tsunamis, which may lead to loss of life and destruction of property. An earthquake is caused by tectonic plates (the making on the earth's crust) getting stuck and putting a strain on the ground. The strain becomes so great that rocks give way and fault lines occur. Earthquakes may occur naturally or as a result of human activities. In its most generic sense, the word earthquake is used to describe any seismic event—whether a natural phenomenon or an event caused by humans—that generates seismic waves.

Causes: Many earthquakes are believed to be caused by tectonic effects, especially the sudden release of accumulated elastic strain energy. Among other possible causes are—sudden shearing accompanying plastic flow, volcanic activity including explosive release of accumulated gas; abrupt volume changes produced by mineral crystallization and polymorphic phase transformations; and abrupt changes in circulation patterns of magma, Rock slides; meteor impacts, and collapse of subsurface caves are other minor causes. Artificial explosions, under or above the surface, also trigger ground motion which at large distances may be difficult (if not impossible) to distinguish from natural earthquakes.

Effects: Earthquakes can produce striking, often highly destructive effects. The intensity of an earthquake is a composite, qualitative measure of the damage to man-made structures and of changes in the surface features of the earth, e.g. visible faults and fissures. It is a measure of the stability of man's structures and of Earth's surfaces. The Mercalli Intensity Scale ranges from degree I, for an earthquake which is felt by a few persons and with no effects on structures, to degree XII, for an earthquake which produces widespread panic, total destruction of buildings, ground accelerations exceeding that of gravity, visible ground motion, and permanent distortion of lines of sight and level. Among the visible effects on earth's surface are: soil slumping, earth avalanches, and water and sand fountains. At sea, the elastic compressional and shear waves are transformed into sound waves when they strike the ocean bottom from beneath. These sound waves are sometimes observed aboard a ship at sea by shaking of the masts and hull (seaquakes). Under special circumstances' an earthquake with focus near or under an ocean, produces a seismic sea wave, known as TSUNAMI. Earthquakes sometimes excite the water in landlocked bays and lakes, which produces an oscillating motion of the water surface, known as a seismic seiche. Frequent earthquakes especially those occurring near areas of alluvial cover, are accompanied and preceded by audible sounds of low pitch. These are triggered by compressional and shear waves in the alluvium, from which, under favorable circumstances, an appreciable sound wave may be transmitted into the air. Most large earthquakes are preceded and followed by a series of smaller shocks, known as foreshocks and aftershocks. A sequence of small earthquakes all occurring in the same region at small time intervals and of the same order of magnitude is known as an earthquake swarm.

Seismic Belts: Earthquakes occur principally in two elongated regions. One passes around the Pacific Ocean (circum-Pacific belt) and includes New Zealand, New Guinea, Japan, the Aleutian Islands, Alaska, and the west coasts of North and South America. It has been estimated that energy released in earthquakes in this region account for 80 per cent of the total earthquake energy release. The other region underlies the Mediterranean region eastward through Asia, passing under the Atlas, Alpine, Iranian, Himalayan, and Burmese Mountains, the island chains of Indonesia and New Guinea, the Solomon Islands, and the New Hebrides. The two regions meet at Celebes. A less active region consists of the Mid-Oceanic Ridges including the submarine mountains underlying the center of the Atlantic, Indian, and South Pacific Oceans.

Depths of Disturbances: Most earthquakes occur at depths of about 25 km; the frequency of occurrence diminishes with depth. The observed depth distribution permits classification into shallow-focus (0-70 km), intermediate-focus (70-300 km), and deep-focus earthquakes (300-700 km). The deepest-focus earthquake on record occurred at about 700 km. The deep-focus types are confined to the circum-Pacific belt. Evidence from analysis of many quakes has suggested that the most common type of earthquakes-producing fault movement is transcurrent -i.e. involving relative horizontal displacement of the two sides of a vertical fault. Such transcurrent faults may be the most important mechanism for shallow-focus disturbances throughout the circum-Pacific belt. Normal fault movements may produce some earthquakes, especially the intermediate-depth ones.

Indian Scenario

Quakes occur more frequently in India because it lies next to the region where the greatest continental collision on Earth is taking place. A hundred million years ago, when dinosaurs roamed the continental masses, the so-called Tethys Sea lay partly between the Indo-Australian and the Eurasian plate. Forty million years later, the Indo-Australian plate collided with the Eurasian plate, neither giving way. The collision is in slow-motion, the closing speed only 2 cm (1 inch) a year, but the energies generated are colossal - the collision area between the two plates has crumpled and pushed upwards to form the Himalayas, the greatest mountain range on the planet. The impact is still being felt and the Himalayas are still rising. Satellite measurements put the ascent of the Himalayas at about 5-millimetres a year.

Seismic Source Delineation

Seismic source delineation is primarily guided by tectonic trends and seismicity. We have made a compilation tectonic features of the region under study, based on "A Generalized tectonic map of India" by Khattri *et al.* (1984), "Tectonic Map of the Himalayan Arc region" by Khattri (1987), "Tectonic Map of India" published by Oil and Natural Gas Commission, "Sketch Map of major tectonic features of south-east Asia" by Leloup *et al.* (1995), the "Map of the Tibetan region" showing fault plane solutions of moderate earthquakes and active faults (Molnar, 1992), and some unpublished material. From seismotectonic considerations the Indian region can be sub-divided into two major provinces, 1) Himalayan arc and other plate boundary regions and 2) the Indian Shield region (S. C. Bhatia, M. Ravi Kumar and H.K. Gupta).

The broad tectonic and seismicity patterns of these regions and the corresponding seismic source zones are described below:

The Indian subcontinent had a long history of devastating earthquakes. The major reason for the high frequency and intensity of the earthquakes is that India continues to drive into Asia at a rate of approximately 47 mm/year. Geographical statistics of India show that almost 54% of the land is vulnerable to earthquakes. The latest version of seismic zoning map of India given in the earthquake resistant design code of India [IS 1893 (Part 1) 2002] assigns four levels of seismicity for entire India in terms of different zone factors. In other words, the earthquake zoning map of India divides India into 5 seismic zones (Zone 1, 2, 3, 4 and 5) unlike its previous version which consisted of five or six zones for the country. According to present zoning map, Zone-5 expects highest level of seismicity whereas Zone-1 & 2 is associated with lowest level of seismicity. The latest seismic zoning map can be accessed from Indian Meteorological Department Website.

Zone-5 is the worst prone zone in the country. It covers the area with the highest risk zone that suffers earthquakes of intensity IX or greater. The IS code assigns zone factor of 0.36 for Zone-5. Structural designer uses this factor for earthquake resistant design of structure in Zone-5.

The zone factor of 0.36 is indicative of effective (zero period) peak horizontal ground accelerations of 0.36 g (36 % of gravity) that may be generated during MCE level earthquake in this zone. It is referred to as the Very High Damage Risk Zone. The state of Kashmir, the western and central Himalayas, the North-East Indian region and the Rann of Kutch fall in this zone.

The Himalayan mountain range is the dramatic outcome of the collision of Indian and Eurasian plates, some 40 million years ago. The Indian plate is still penetrating deeper at an estimated rate of about 5 cm/year. The Himalayan collision zone has been marked by intense seismic activity. Four great earthquakes (1897 Assam, 1905 Kangra, 1934 Bihar-Nepal and 1950 Assam) occurred here in a short span of 53 years. The frequent moderate earthquakes and the infrequent great earthquakes suggest that episodic slippage is a continuous process.

These ongoing processes also imply that in future great earthquakes can be expected in the unruptured parts of the Himalayan front. Major uncertainties remain regarding the recurrence interval of great earthquakes.

Zone-4 is called the High Damage Risk Zone and covers areas liable to Intensity VIII. The IS code assigns zone factor of 0.24 for Zone-4. The Indo-Gangetic basin and the Rajasthan region fall in Zone-4.

Zone-3: The Andaman and Nicobar Islands, parts of Kashmir, Western Himalayas and Punjab fall under this zone. This zone is classified as Moderate Damage Risk Zone which is liable to Intensity VII. The IS code assigns zone factor of 0.16 for Zone-3.

Zone-1 & 2: This region is liable to Intensity VI or less and is classified as the Low Damage Risk Zone. The IS code assigns zone factor of 0.10 (maximum horizontal acceleration that can be experienced by a structure in this zone is 10 % of gravitational acceleration) for Zone-1 & 2.

Development of Seismicity Programme

The first seismological observatory in the country was established in Alipur (Calcutta) in 1898. Subsequently, two more observatories were established at Colaba (Bombay) and Madras in 1899 (later shifted to Kodaikanal). The national network was further expanded by the Indian Meteorological Department (IMD). In December 1967, an observatory was established at the National Geophysical Research Institute (NGRI), Hyderabad.

The IMD is the national organization maintaining the national seismological network, providing information on earthquakes to the Government and the media. Institutions like the Bhabha Atomic Research Center (BARC) and the NGRI also carry out earthquake monitoring and research.

The Global Positioning System (GPS) measures the time required from an orbiting satellite to a ground receiver and converts this time to distance. A receiver on the ground makes measurements, with a clock that is time-synchronized with an orbiting GPS satellite equipped with atomic clock. The central core of the operation is the simultaneous determination of distances between a ground station and sets of four or more satellites. The distance between a satellite and receiver is calculated by comparing the time of GPS signal reception with the time of transmission. Simultaneous measurement of the distances to four satellites is required to solve for the receiver's position on the Earth's surface in terms of latitude, longitude and height. By repeating these measurements over discrete time intervals, change in station coordinates can be determined to a high degree of precision. By repeated observations and using different data processing techniques, changes between the baselines can be determined.

Anjar Earthquake 1956

People living in the industrial township of Anjar, 34 miles from Bhuj were probably enjoying their dinner or were already asleep when an earthquake rocked it. On 21st July 1956 since most of 20,000-odd residents were indoors the impact of the quake was intensified.

As buildings crumbled 115 died, over half the population were rendered homeless, more than 3,000 houses in 25 villages developed huge cracks, losses ran upto Rs. 1 crore. Such devastation wreaked by the quake made it one of the worst calamities to hit Kutch in the past 100 years.

The quake also resulted in a landslide, which dislocated railway services and snapped communication and telegraph lines. Anjar, which was known for manufacturing knives and nutcrackers and was considered the industrial center of Kutch till the government decided to develop Kutch as a major port, suddenly witnessed mass migration.

Over 8,000 affected people migrated from the district a few days after the quake. Rains added to the misery of thousands living in temporary camps.

Table 5.0

Date	Event	Magnitude	Max. Intensity	Deaths
June 1819	Kutch	8.3	IX	1,500
June 1897	Assam	8.7	XII	1,500
February 1900	Coimbatore	6.0	VII	Not Known
April 1905	Kangra	8.0	X	19,000
January 1934	Bihar-Nepal	8.3	X	11,000
August 1950	Assam	8.6	XII	1,530
July 1956	Anjar	6.1	IX	115
December 1967	Koyna	6.5	VIII	125
March 1970	Bharuch	5.2	VII	30
January 1975	Kinnaur	6.8	VIII	200
August 1988	Bihar-Nepal	6.8	IX	1,000
October 1991	Uttarkashi	6.4	IX	768
September 1993	Killari (Latur)	6.2	VIII	7,928
May 1997	Jabalpur	6.0	VIII	39
March 1999	Chamoli	6.8	VIII	103
January 2001	Bhuj	7.7	X	13,805
December 2004	Indian Ocean Earthquake	9.1	XI	2,30,210 (All over World)

Koyna Earthquake (1967)

A powerful quake-measuring 6.5 on the Richter Scale-shook Koyna, about 115 kilometers from Poona, on December 11, 1967, claiming over 125 lives and injuring more than 1,400.

It will remain etched in the collective memories of the people of Maharashtra for several reasons. To date, it remains one of the most powerful quakes to ever rock Maharashtra.

Survivors had to undergo further trauma as aftershocks and tremors rocked the area for two more days. Bombay recorded 43 tremors, while Poona registered 100 aftershocks. Buildings in the

Bombay-Poona belt developed cracks. Building collapses caused most deaths in the Koyna quake; hence, during these two days of aftershocks, there were several reports of citizens rushing out of their homes on to the roads at the slightest hint of a tremor.

The quake almost paralysed Maharashtra as it affected the operations of Koyna power plant. While the plant did not suffer any major damage, it needed some minor repairs and maintenance that resulted in industrial units in Western Maharashtra and Bombay suffering from power blackout for days on end.

In fact, textile mills, the backbone of Bombay's financial world in those days, had to cut down on work. For instance, 65 mills in Bombay decided to stagger work, with half the number of mills working on alternate days.

Kinnaur Earthquake (1975)

This struck in the early afternoon of January 19, 1975. It caused disasters in parts of the Kinnaur, Lahaul and Spiti regions of India. Seismographers think that the movements along the Kaurik Fault caused this earthquake to occur which killed hundreds of people and cause severe damage of property. Two massive landslides took place during the earthquake. One of them was near Maling in the Spiti Valley. The other one blocked the Paro-chu River near Sumdo. This earthquake caused many smaller occurrences of slope failure. Communications failed and helicopters were used to bring relief. The magnitude of this earthquake was about 6.8 on the Richter Scale.

Bihar Earthquake (1988)

Earthquake that struck 21 August 1988 could not have come at a worst time for the state. It had barely recovered from the news of a steamer capsizing in the Ganga off Maniharighat with 400 people aboard a fortnight earlier. The quake - 6.8 on the Richter Scale-killed over 850 people and left 15,000 injured in Bihar, the Himalayan region and Nepal. It struck in two installments of 10 seconds and 15 seconds each, yet it managed to leave cracks in 50,000 buildings, including Raj Bhavan and the old

Secretariat Building, in Bihar. In fact, the then Bihar governor G.N. Singh had to move to the ground floor of the building because his residence had suffered damages. Bhootahi Balan River breached an embankment in Madhubani district and inundated various areas. In short, Bihar villages turned into ruins.

Uttarkashi Earthquake (1991)

This earthquake took place in the early morning of October 20, 1991. This earthquake was so severe that it shook most parts of Uttarkashi and Chamoli districts of Garhwal.

This earthquake was very severe and caused damage to a lot of lives and property. The communication system was destroyed and the region was cut off from the rest of the world due to the debris. Landslides also occurred at many locations. The magnitude of the earthquake was about 6.4 on the Richter Scale.

Latur Earthquake (1993)

Darkness descended at dawn in Latur and Osmanabad districts of Maharashtra on September 30, 1993. A quake measuring about 6.2 on the Richter Scale, with its epicenter in the Killari village of Latur, killed about 12,000 people and injured as many.

Latur and Osmanabad lie in the seismic zone, and villagers here are no strangers to quakes, but the magnitude of devastation shocked all. A flashback to 1993 would reveal street corners turning into crematoria and burial grounds. Death was so rampant that in some cases four to five bodies had to be piled on the same platform for cremation. In many areas, the military and its earthmovers were busy locating people trapped under debris. Such mentally crippling sights left many survivors traumatized. In fact, social scientists had then stated that it would take years for the survivors to recover.

Unofficial figures put the toll at 35,000. Later on, five

community buildings providing a range of amenities were unveiled at Chincholikate. The buildings were meant for an animal shelter, a gram panchayat, a women's center, a Samaj Mandir and a childcare center. Both the housing and community center together cost Rs 2.25 crore.

Jabalpur Earthquake (1997)

This earthquake took a toll of 39 human lives and caused extensive damage of property. The damage was maximum in Jabalpur and Mandla districts of Madhya Pradesh, but lesser in Chindwara and Sirni districts. A total of 8267 houses collapsed and more than 40,000 were partially damaged. This earthquake attains significance because it was near to an urban conglomeration.

Chamoli Earthquake (1999)

The Chamoli district of Uttarakhand witnessed on early hours of 29 March, 1999, this earthquake causing extensive damage to property and loss of 103 lives.

Effects of earthquake were seen in six districts Chamoli, Rudraprayag, Tihari Garhwal, Bagheswar, Uttarkashi and Pauri Garhwal.

Gujarat Earthquake (2001)

In the towns and villages of Kutch, which were reduced to rubble on January 26, 2001, most survivors were eating out of relief kitchens and living in makeshift camps. When rescue attempts were deemed futile and relief had reached even remote corners, it was time for the trickiest phase long-term rehabilitation.

It is estimated that five towns-Bhuj, Bhachao, Anjar, Rapar and Gandhidham and about 400 villages will require a helping hand. Houses, schools and health centers need to be rebuilt quickly, while issues relating to orphans, post-disaster trauma and the environment have to be tackled.

The Bhuj Earthquake most seriously affected 'Kandla Port' the busiest port of India. The economic losses reported as follows in several categories (in US $ million)-

Loss of personal properties- 82

Loss of household properties- 2,382

Loss of public utilities- 27

Loss of public infrastructure and amenities- 230

Loss of industrial establishment- 1,060

Loss of commercial establishment- 638

Total loss about- 4419 $ million.

The physical damage is apparent but the human cost is yet to be counted with thousands of people killed and injured and whole communities wiped out.

"Indian National Day will long be remembered as a day of Sorrow."

Towards this end, the Gujarat government recently announced that it would soon unveil a revival package for industries ravaged by the devastating earthquake. This, he hoped, would boost the fund-raising effort and help in quick collection of the sum of Rs. 20,000 crores necessary to rehabilitate the state. Foreign participation in the rehabilitation work, too, would get a boost with this move, he added.

Indian Ocean Earthquake (2004)

That severe earthquake struck the North Indian Ocean and the Bay of Bengal. Nearly 2,30,210 people were estimated to have been killed in wide Tsunami generated by this earthquake. Nicobar Island and to a lesser extent the Andaman Islands, were hardest hit territory in India with as many as 4,486 deaths. Extensive damage occurred in the Nicobar Island due to the Tsunami that is estimated to have attained heights of as much as 20-meters at places.

However, by virtue of its economic sizes, the immediate and medium-term impact on economic growth is proportionately much greater in Sri Lanka and Maldives than in Thailand, Indonesia and India. The region's financial markets remained 'Strangely serene' (EIU 2005). Currencies have not been collapsed, and in Sri Lanka massive aid commitments triggered a significant appreciation of the nominal exchange rate. The main reason for the limited economic impact was that the tsunami missed the industrial and commercial centers of all affected countries other than Maldives.

CHAPTER 6

Developing an Asian Tsunami Warning System

NARESH KUMAR VERMA
Political Geography Division,
S.I.S, Jawaharlal Nehru University, New Delhi.

Introduction

The waves of the Asian Tsunami[1] of 2004 that hit countries of South and South-east Asia were triggered by an earthquake measuring 9.0 on the Richter scale.[2] The Tsunami waves devastated coastal regions of Indonesia, Malaysia, Thailand, Myanmar, India, Sri Lanka, Maldives and even reaching as far as Somalia in Africa. Conservative estimates suggested that around 250,000 people lost their lives, while injuring millions. This makes it one of the worst natural disasters the world has ever seen.

This paper takes a look at the attempts to build the Tsunami Warning System in the Asian continent following the disaster. It will also examine how such systems have been functioning in other parts of the world- in particular the Pacific Tsunami Warning System and the Japan Meteorological Agency's Tsunami Warning Service. Their experience can prove useful for such system here. Role of the UN too will be examined. Finally, given India's prominent role in the region, it can definitely bring in its expertise to develop such a system and effectively operationalise it. The underlying argument here will be that for effective functioning of such a mechanism, countries of the region will need to shed their differences and work together so that loss resulting from such catastrophes could be minimised.

Asian Tsunami Warning System

The Tsunami and the earthquake that triggered it are natural phenomena. While earthquakes cannot be forecast they can be quickly pinpointed. Moreover, if the appropriate scientific equipment is in place, the formation of a Tsunami can also be detected and its likely path predicted and even tracked. For decades now, Japan and countries of the Pacific Ocean have been running a Tsunami Early Warning System, saving precious lives and economic resources. In the wake of the disaster, countries of the region explored ways to better deal with such situations in the future. On the top of their agenda was the Tsunami Early Warning System. An analysis of the events on the day of the Tsunami suggested that even if people in the way of water have been informed of the impending waves, the casualty figure could have been substantially less.[1] None of the countries in the region had a Tsunami warning mechanism or even tidal gauges to alert the people of the impending Tsunami waves.[2] With this aspect in mind, countries of the region got together to set up such a system. With two meetings in Japan and Indonesia in 2005, the countries began to thrash out the idea. Yet they were unable to agree upon who should run the system. India, Indonesia and Thailand wanted to take the control of the system in their hands and therefore had pledged resources for such a centre. However, other countries did not agree with them. Finally, United Nations took matters in its hands as a coordinator for the system.

The underlying problem in working out the modalities of such a system was the willingness on the part of the countries in the region to share sensitive data among themselves. Working with the notions of national sovereignty, they were unwilling to enter a cooperative framework despite the huge losses and casualties suffered. This is one of the reasons why India, Indonesia and Thailand wanted to take control of the system in their hands, so as not to take any risks. However, as the following section suggests the concerns of the Asian countries are unfounded because such a system has been working in the Pacific region and that too effectively.

Working of the Pacific Tsunami Warning System

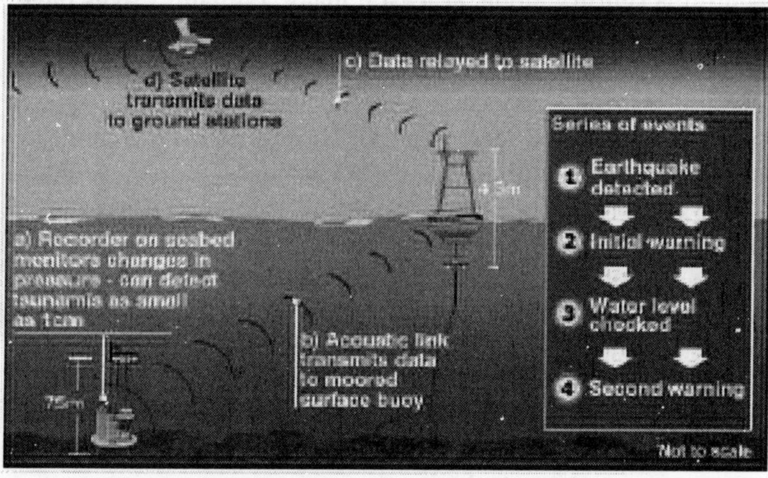

1. Seismic observatories in the region detect an earthquake and send data to the Pacific Tsunami Warning Center in Hawaii.

2. If the earthquake is in the Pacific basin and above 7.5 on Richter scale, an initial "Tsunami watch" alert is sent out.

3. Data from monitoring stations deep on the seabed near the earthquake's epicentre is checked for signs of a tsunami.

4. If a tsunami is detected, full warnings are sent out via national systems which have been set up in several countries.

Japan's Experience in Tsunami Warning System

In putting up the Tsunami Warning System, Asian countries can definitely take help of Japan. It has one of the most populated coastal regions in the world and a long history of earthquake activity. In fact, in the aftermath of the Asian Tsunami, Japan was one of the leading developed nations to deploy its troops for rescue and relief operations. Its deployment was one of the largest. It also offered $ 500 million to help Tsunami victims. Keeping in mind its own experience, Japan's humanitarian assistance was one of the largest.[4]

In this century alone, at least 6 major Tsunami waves have destroyed entire coastal populations in Japan. Keeping in mind the dangers posed by Tsunamis, Tokyo had established the Tsunami Warning Service in 1952.[5] The service is run by the Japan Meteorological Society (JMA). This centre further connects 6 regional centres equipped with 300 sensors. These sensors are located across Japan's islands, including around 80 water-borne sensors, monitor seismic activity round the clock. Whenever there is a danger of Tsunami, local authorities, central government and disaster relief organisations get warnings through special channels so that they can handle the emergency. For general public, the alerts are broadcasted on all radio and TV channels, and if necessary an evacuation warning is also given. This warning and alert are given at least 10 minutes before so that people can evacuate the area.

The technical expertise of the JMA's has been proven with success. Its sophistication is such that the agency can predict the height, speed, destination and even the arrival time of any tsunami destined for Japanese shores. However, this technical accuracy does come at a price. JMA's Tsunami Warning Service costs around US $ 20 million to the Japanese exchequer.

Pacific Tsunami Warning System

After Japan, another system that can prove useful for Asian nations is the Pacific Tsunami Warning System. The system has been constructed in the Pacific Ocean in the late 1940s. With continuous upgradations, the system has been performing smoothly. The system consists of the seismological instruments that register tremors, a network of sea level gauges and deep-sea sensors or "tsunameters" linked by satellite to round-the-clock monitoring stations based in Hawaii, Alaska and Japan. Using computer modelling, scientists can predict the likely propagation of tsunamis and their probable impact.

Another important part of the system is the Deep Assessment and Reporting of Tsunamis (DART). DART is composed of two parts: a sea floor sensor and a buoy that relays Tsunami information to warning centres on the ground by satellite communication.[6]

Components of an Asian Tsunami Warning System

In a Tsunami warning system, Seismographs provide the first line of defence, alerting monitoring staff to any earthquakes large enough to produce a tsunami. But not every such quake produces these deadly waves, so tidal

Such system has been put in place 18 months after the disaster struck, but problems remain. The system is being overseen by UNESCO's Intergovernmental Oceanographic Commission.[8] In this system, there are 26 national tsunami information centres receiving information from 25 new seismographic stations. There are also three deep-ocean sensors to detect and report tsunamis. As already noted, for any Tsunami warning system to be effective, there has to be an open and free exchange of data and the full interoperability of national systems. This is absolutely crucial for success.

India's Role

In this context, India's role becomes significant. When the Tsunami waves struck the region, India had played a major role in the rescue and relief operations. The Indian naval ships, aircraft, helicopters, and personnel responded to the crisis situation promptly. The Indian Navy deployed 32 naval ships, seven aircraft and 20 helicopters in support of five rescue, relief and reconstruction missions as part of 'Operation Madad' (Andhra Pradesh and Tamil Nadu coast), 'Operation Sea Waves' (Andaman & Nicobar Islands), 'Operation Castor' (Maldives), 'Operation Rainbow' (Sri Lanka) and 'Operation Gambhir' (Indonesia). On 26 December 2004, the day Tsunami hit the subcontinent, the Indian Navy had deployed 19 ships, four aircraft, and 11 helicopters that rushed to Maldives, Sri Lanka and Tamil Nadu and Andaman & Nicobar Islands. This speaks volumes of the efficiency and the operational readiness of the

Indian Navy.[3] This also brings to fore what major role India can play in the regional Tsunami warning system.

The system that India proposes to install in the Indian Ocean will be the first stage of an overall approach to the disaster management system.[9] The Indian government plans to spear-head a system that would be linked across South Asia. This is a positive development because India as a developing nation should take an initiative in this regard.

India currently has 20 deep-sea buoys with sensors in the Bay of Bengal and Arabian Sea. But they are not equipped with the pressure sensors needed for advance warning of giant tsunamis. For such a warning system to come in effect, India needs to add 20 more of these buoys. These buoys also need to be placed at important points where the plates collided.[2] It will also deploy between six and twelve Deep Ocean Assessment and Reporting Systems (DOARS), about six kilometers below the sea surface. The entire project is estimated to cost around US $ 27 million and take two and a half years to complete.

India also plans to liaise with countries in South-East Asia- such as Indonesia, Myanmar and Thailand- that already have the software for such warning systems, and will share data with its South Asian neighbours. Such an advance warning system will be useful only if there is a system of getting the information across to local communities in time.

To be truly effective, however any Tsunami warning system should be a part of an overall disaster reduction strategy. This is because coastal population faces danger not only from Tsunamis but also from earthquakes and cyclones.

Conclusion

In conclusion it can be said that, for the effective Tsunami warning system, countries of the region should join hands together to save the region from another such calamity. Even though the probability of such a calamity taking place in the region are less, the countries should nonetheless be prepared to deal with the situation in a better manner.

References

1. According to one of the estimates, the Tsunami reached beaches of Phuket and coasts of Sri Lanka two hours after the earthquake. Had there been early warning, it would have given enough time to the people to reach higher ground. See National Institute of Advanced Industrial Science and Technology. "Tsunamis in the Indian Ocean from Sumatra Earthquake", available at http://staff.aist.go.jp/kenji.satake/Sumatra-E.html.
2. See "USGS: Warnings Could Have Saved Thousands in Asia", *Reuters* report dated 26th December 2004.
3. From http://news.bbc.co.uk/2/hi/asia-pacific/4190375.htm
4. Lam Peng Er, "Japan's Human Security Role in South-east Asia", *Contemporary South-east Asia*, Vol. 28, 2006.
5. http://www.unisdr.org/ppew/tsunami/what-is-tsunami/backinfor-tsunami-ws.htm.
6. Charles W. Schmidt, "Natural Disasters: Building a Tsunami Warning System", *Environmental Health Perspectives*, Vol. 113, No. 2, February 2005, p. A90.
7. Will Knight, "Tsunami warning system is not simply sensors".
8. http://www.newscientist.com/article.ns?id=dn6839.
   http://news.bbc.co.uk/2/hi/asia-pacific/5126710.htm.
9. Vijay Sakhuja, "Indian Naval Diplomacy: Post Tsunami", *IPCS article* dated 8th February 2006, www.ipcs.org.
10. During the Tsunami, an estimated 1,200 km of faultline slipped about 15 m along the subduction zone where the India Plate slides under the Burma Plate. The India plate carries the Nicobar Islands, the Andaman Islands and northern Sumatra.

CHAPTER 7

Disaster Management in India

DR. L.K. RAO

Lecturer of Geography, Govt. College, Bhiwani.

Introduction

The country is struck by one form of tragedy or the other quite frequently. It could be a devastating super cyclone, a killer earthquake, flood or drought and rarely a Tsunami. Experience shows that the official response in such calamities is invariably inadequate and relief operations are poorly managed. This gives a reflection that we are insensitive to human sufferings. The poor and have-nots suffer the most during a calamity. They are left in the lurch both by God and lesser god of today's India.

I would like to give you introduction of Disaster Management Programme in India. Perhaps very few peoples know that the National Institute for Disaster Management was set up in Bhopal in 1987 at the prompting of the late Prime Minister Rajiv Gandhi following Bhopal Gas tragedy.

Secondly the Ministry of agriculture has a full fledged unit called Natural Disaster Management Division, which is supposed to manage natural disasters and coordinate relief operations. The Indian Meteorological Deptt. (IMD) also has a separate division for cyclone warning. It gives warning through AIR and Doordarshan.

Indian Scenario in the Context of Disasters

India is one of the most disaster prone countries in the world. This is due to its geographical location and geological formation. The prevailing climatological conditions over the Indian continent surrounded by long coastal lines, high mountain ranges, snow clad mountains perennial rivers in the North, the Brahmaputra, Gangetic river system, all add to the problem. India which has 20% of the world land area has to support around 16% of the human population and also a large number of cattle population which heavily depend on the forest area.

The forest cover with more than 0.4 density is 12% of the land area though forest area is under 23%. The NRSA satellite coverage shows only 12% coverage of good forest area. Due to degraded forest and compacted mud, the water percolation and the water holding capacity is less which leads to soil erosion during monsoon, and silting of rivers. The intense rainfall during monsoon resulting in more than 100 cm rain in 36 hours or getting the whole monsoon rain for two to three days like the one which is received by the western region and particularly in Mumbai it is becoming very common and frequent. If we analyse region wise, the Northern India is confronted by Avalanches, landslides, floods, drought and earthquake as most of the area fall under seismic zone III to V.

The Eastern region is affected by severe flood due to Brahmaputra and Gangetic rivers. Drought, heavy winds, heat waves, hailstorm, cyclone and earthquakes are also common. The North-Eastern region is also affected by floods, landslides and wind damage and also the earthquakes as most of the area fall under seismic zone IV and V.

The Western region is known for severe drought, wind erosion of sand and soil, floods, cyclone (in Gujarat area) and also prone to earthquake (Bhuj).

In the Southern region, the Coromandal coast is vulnerable to cyclone, sea erosion, tsunami and landsliding in hilly areas. The island of Andaman and Nicobar are prone to sea erosion and tsunami.

Out of total 600 districts nearly 80 districts are coastal and prone to sea erosion, sea level rise, cyclones and rarely a tsunami. More than 100 districts are hilly in the North, North-east, Eastern Ghats and Western Ghats and are prone to landslides. More than 250 districts are included under DPAP (Drought Prone Area Programme) and also under DDP (Desert Development Programme).

Nearly 40 million hectares area is generally prone to flood which is very frequent as a result large size of population gets displaced. This is very common in U.P., Bihar, West Bengal, Assam and Orissa. It is quite ironical that the highest rainfall area Cherapunji in Meghalaya is also facing the problem of drought and water scarcity. Indian coastal regions have also faced some of the severest cyclones both in Eastern Coast and Western coast in Gujarat.

One of the natural disasters namely the volcanoes are in Barren island i.e. Andaman group of island. It becomes active periodically and in 2005 also became very active. Since long time, Nobody has heard about tsunami. On 26th Jan 2004, tsunami had its devastating impact in Tamil Nadu, Andamans, Kerala and Andhra Pradesh.

Major Disasters of India in the last two decades

Uttarkashi Earthquake	1991
Latur Earthquake	1993
Chamouli Earthquake	1999
Orissa Super Cyclone	1999
Bhuj Earthquake	2001
Tsunami	2004
Bombay-Gujarat Flood	2005
Barmer Flood	2006

In addition we also confronted the Bhopal gas tragedy and plague in Gujarat.

Impacts of Disasters

The direct impact of disaster is death, injury to people and animal population and also destruction of properties. Everything i.e., support system, namely communication, power supply,. water supply, drainage etc. goes haywire. The healthcare and hospitals are also put under severe stress. All the economic activities came to a standstill. Peoples livelihood especially of poor and vulnerable are badly affected for a long time till normalcy returns. The psychological trauma of the disaster is very high and people go through the trauma for a long time.

Responsible Mechanism and Action Taken by Government

Disaster is a state subject and it is the primary responsibility of the State Govt. of India to facilitate and extend support financial and other through various ministries. In the state there is a specific apparatus namely the Relief Commissioner or Disaster Management Secretary and also a state level Disaster Management Committee, consisting of senior secretary of various departments and representatives from NGO's at the district level and it is chaired by D.C. with all departments heads and member of NGO's such as Red Cross etc. These committees meet periodically before the onset of the monsoon and also on the event of any major disaster. These committees can also take help from CRPF and defence services whenever required.

The Union Govt. plays a significant role in disaster management to states and assist them with all the required supports like Defence services, air dropping, searching, transport of relief goods, health personnel and medical support. At national level there is a Crisis Management Committee headed by cabinet secretaries and all other major departmental secretaries. There is a Control Relief Commissions in the Home Ministry which coordinates with all the ministers. There is a division under Home Ministry i.e. National Disaster Management division. The Home Ministry is the nodal Ministry for all disaster except drought which is under Agriculture Ministry. The Govt. of India set up a powered committee on Disaster Management in Aug. 1999 under the leadership of J.C.Pant.

Disaster Management

A calamity relief fund has been constituted with the contribution of Central Govt. and respective state Govt. in the ratio of 3:1. The 12th finance commission has recommended Rs. 23,000/- crores assistance for the period. If any disaster of severe nature occurs, the state prepares a memorandum and present to the Home Ministry. A central team visits the affected area of the state and a report is prepared. The report is presented before the High level committee which decides the quantum of assistance and the fund is released. The Calamity Relief Fund (CRF) has been made eligible only for the following types of disasters.

Cyclone, drought, flood, earthquake, fire, hailstorm, landslide, avalanches, cloud burst and pest attack. With all the above mentioned committees and recommendations, the past experience shows that official response in such calamities is invariably inadequate and relief operations are slipshod. This reflects poor system which gives the impression of being insensitive to human sufferings.

I would like to quote from the Tribune dated Nov. 5, 1999. After his aerial survey of Orissa's cyclone hit areas along with Union Home Minister L. K. Advani, Defence Minister George Fernandes said, "The centre is drawing up the framework of a formed disaster management setup to deal with the crisis". Nothing can be more shameful than the absence of a well coordinated system which should know how to work on a war footing during the natural disasters. Everything should be automatic once the disaster signal is switched on.

It will be worthwhile to quote Davinder Kumar's report in Indian Express Oct. 31, 1999. "In an age of super computers, satellite phones and cutting edge technologies, the Natural Disaster Management Division of the Govt. did nothing more than coordinating and evacuating the people from coastal areas. The respective State Govt. followed the same drill waiting for the devastation to happen.

This is of course a larger issue which needs to be thoroughly debated at national level. We ought to learn from other countries which have revamped their setups so as to act in time and effectively to minimise the human sufferings.

I wish to quote from Times of India concerning the warning system developed by the University of Lisbon to trace an earthquake prone zone, "It is a well coordinated system which can pick up seismic waves in 25 seconds, it takes only 10 seconds. For Lisbon to send a warning to the civil authorities directly or indirectly, and 15 seconds before the earthquake hit the city. This centre has enough time to switch off the city's gas and power system."

We can surely learn from other countries experience and seek the help of International Agencies to update our disaster management technology in various areas.

A thoroughly professional and efficient response system holds the key to satisfactory disaster management. We need a coordinated system of disaster Management with human touch.

Conclusion

Thus, many disaster management plan exists in India but it seems that its effectiveness is limited because of inadequate staff and resources. It is not true that the Indians are not capable of managing crisis situations. We have the basic infrastructure as well as the technology to properly monitor the signals from disaster prone zones but in the absence of modern technological backup, serious gaps have appeared in the way, reflecting how poorly the various governmental agencies function. Moreover the attitude of the machinery also matters greatly in this case. Official apathy can be seen everywhere. According to a psychology expert, "the general impression that Indians are incompetent at crisis management have something to do with their attitude." In such matters everything flows from the response system at the official level.

CHAPTER 8

Ground Water Depletion in South-west Haryana

DR. R.N. YADAV

Department of Geography, GVMGRR College, Ch. Dadri (Haryana).

The arid and semi-arid areas which are marked by annual/seasonal deficit of moisture the means of irrigation are must for the proper growth of crops. Apart from paucity of rain water in absolute terms, such areas also suffer from higher variability of precipitation from year to year. In such circumstances there are two options for agricultural development firstly to evolve suitable dry farming techniques and secondly to make provision for the very slow pace of recharge of ground water in semi-arid areas, the irrigation methods need to be designed accordingly. In this paper an attempt has been made to analyse and assess the socio-economic life of the people due to depletion of ground water.

Methodology and Source of Data

The study is based on intensive field work of all the 622 households of the village. A questionnaire was used to collect the required information. The data was collected then processed and subsequently represented by suitable tables, maps and diagrams. During field work social data on age, sex, caste, literacy, housing condition and economic data on occupational structure, land holding, type of irrigation, cropping pattern, livestock, income and expenditure of the families were collected. Village cadastral maps were used to represent the cropping and land-use pattern.

Origin of the Village

According to the records of 'Jaga' Satyanarain this village was founded by Yadavs of Chora Gotra. The 'Jaga' records tell us that the Chora gotra ancestor was Harpal Singh, the ruler of Ajmer. He was defeated by King Peerm Saha. Harpal Singh ran away to save himself from the soldiers of Peerm Saha. He took shelter in dense forest near Narnaul town known as Kaimla Johad forest. Harpal Singh lived for a long time in this dense forest of Kaimla and was married in Vikram Samvat 921. Bikha Ram and Rattan Singh were two grandson of Harpal who founded village Bikhawali on the name of Bikhawali in Baisakh Badi 2, Samvat 1115. With the passage of time Bikhawali village renamed as 'Bhankhri'.

Irrigation Techniques Used in the Village 'Bhankhri'

Before the advent of tube-well irrigation in the village in the mid 1970s, charsa was the main method of irrigation. Under this method water was drawn from the wells using a large leather bag tied to a large rope. This method was labour intensive, time consuming and quite inefficient. The studied area had a very small proportion of cultivated areas i.e., less than 2 per cent was irrigated before the period of tube well irrigation. With the availability of cheap hydroelectricity to the village in 1975, as well as the diffusion of high yielding varieties of seeds the farmers of the village opted to go for tube well irrigation in a big way. In 1975 only two tube wells were installed. The number of tube wells increased rapidly and it had gone upto about 90 in early 1980s. As a result, the proportion of irrigated areas also increased from 2 per cent in 1970 to 75 per cent in 1980-81. In 1974-75 the intensity of irrigation was 20 per cent while in 1980-81 it was 60 per cent and 2005-06 it was only 10 per cent. The intensity of irrigation also effects the intensity of cropping. In 1974-75 the intensity of cropping was 129 while in 1980-81 it was 171 and in 2004-05 it again decreased to 120. Despite installation of tube wells in the village during 1975-80, the ground water table had also registered perceptible rise. It was due to the damming of Dohan stream by Haryana Government in 1978. The rise in water table further encouraged the farmers to install more tube wells. In 1980s the depth of ground water was 50 to 70 feet.

With the passage of time the ground water dwindled rapidly due to firstly damming of Dohan stream by Rajasthan Government in 1980-81 at a distance of about 30 kilometers upstream of Bhankhri village resulting in sharp decline in the rate of ground water recharge in the study areas and secondly continual draft of ground water by a large number of tube wells installed in the village since 1975.

The problem of ground water depletion came to be felt perceptibly by the mid 1980s in terms of decreasing water pressure in tube wells. Slowly and gradually the tube wells started running out of water working a few hours at a stretch. The ground water table receded further and further down and by the end of the 1980s the tube wells began to go out of operation. Consequently with the passage of time the village came to be characterized by acute water scarcity. Even drinking water had to be fetched from other neighboring village named Khatoti located at a distance of 2 kilometers at the bank of Dohan river. The cost of installing deep tube wells was so high that small and marginal farmer could not afford it. Thus, the depletion of ground water resource had resulted in both water supply problems as well as water management problems (AL-Saleh, 1992, P.220). By 1992 most of the tube wells had gone dry and the village came in for bad days, both in economic and social terms. At present there is no ground water availability upto of 1000 feet.

Impact on Cropping Pattern

The changing availability of irrigation water affects the

cropping pattern of the village. The main impact of increase and decrease in irrigation was on the rabi crops as winter season is virtually without any rainfall except a very scantly cyclonic rain fall in the area. In the pre-irrigation period gram was the main crop followed by sarson and barley in terms of acreage. With the introduction of tube wells irrigation in the mid 1970s area under wheat registered rapid increase making it soon the first ranking rabi crop. The increase in wheat acreage was at the cost of gram crop which decline to second rank among the rabi crops. With the depletion of ground water, wheat slipped down to lower rank. In the same way the acreage of fallow land has also gone up quite high again. In other words, the cropping pattern has returned almost to the same, as it was in early 1970s. With the decrease of irrigation intensity the sarson, cash crop has acquired less moisture as well as labour than the wheat crop which was at the first rank during the high irrigation intensity period. The change in emphasis from wheat to sarson in the rabi session is closely related to the decline in animal population since mid 1970s; as against the pre 1975 period, the village now has a much smaller number of animals and thus there is a considerable reduced requirement for fodder as compared to that in the earlier period. Consequently sarson cultivation gets preference over wheat which to a large extent was grown for fodder earlier. The increase in sarson cultivation after the depletion at ground water has also adversely affected the areas under bajra in the kharif season. As after the bajra crop the soil is not left with adequate moisture for proper growth of sarson crop so the farmers prefer to forgo the former to get the latter cash crop.

The extension of irrigation did not make perceptible difference in the cropping pattern of the kharif season. There was no change in the relative ranking at the top three kharif crops i.e., bajra, guar and jowar. The area under bajra and jowar has gradually come down between 1974-75 and 2004-05 (Table 8.0).

Ranking of Crops

Table 8.0 : Village Bhankhri

(1970-71) Pre-irrigation period			*(1985-86) Irrigation Period*			*(2004-05) Post-Irrigation period*		
Rabi	*Rank*	*Kharif*	*Rabi*	*Rank*	*Kharif*	*Rabi*	*Rank*	*Kharif*
Gram	1	Bajra	Wheat	1	Bajra	Sarson	1	Bajra
Sarson	2	Guar	Gram	2	Guar	Gram	2	Bajra
Barley	3	Jowar	Sarson	3	Jowar	Wheat	3	Jowar
Wheat	4		Barley	4		Barley	4	

Source : Based on Lal Kitab and Field Work

Impact on Livestock

The village is facing acute water scarcity since the last one decade even for drinking purpose. When the drinking water for humans and animals has to be fetched from the adjoining villages, it had naturally become difficult to support a large cattle population as in the previous years. Consequently the number of animals which had gone up considerably during the heyday of tube wells irrigation have come down gradually (Table 8.1.)

The decline in number of drought animals like bullocks, camels and donkeys was remarkable in view of the rise in the number of tractors. The village also witnessed fall in all categories of livestock including the milch cattle. This reflects that the worsening agriculture conditions in the wake of

Table 8.1 : Livestock in Bhankhri Village (1975-2005)

Year	*Cows*	*Buffaloes*	*Bullocks*	*Camels*	*Donkeys*	*Goats*	*Sheep*
1975	140	239	80	50	30	102	70
1985	100	254	62	42	24	110	80
1995	40	210	05	12	10	90	20
2005	10	140	Nil	07	8	50	10

Source : Based on Field work, 2004-05

depletion of ground water resource in the village have also made an adverse impact on cattle population.

Change in Tree Cover

The period of tube wells irrigation also witnessed large scale of trees in the village mainly due to the following reasons : (i) Tractorization of agriculture which came in the wake of the extension of tube wells irrigation, worked to stop growth of new seedling through greater frequency of deep ploughing in the fields. The farmers had also cut down many trees which hindered unobstructed and easy mobility of tractors in the field. (ii) Land consolidation in the late 1960 had also made its own contribution in the removal of trees in the fields. Each household had cut down many of trees on their land which was likely to be allotted to someone else. (iii) The depletion of ground water also effects the growth of trees and due to increasing depth of ground water a large number of tree in field and on roadsides dried. (iv) The decline in the number of wild animals like deer and 'neelgai' further added to the problem of decline number of jand trees as the jand seeds do not germinate if these have not passed through the digestive system of these animals.

Change in Lifestyle of Villagers

Before the commencement of tube wells irrigation general thrift and limited consumption was a hall mark of the people in the village. Even tea taking was quite uncommon in the village before the commencement of tube wells irrigation and people generally happened to take it when on a visit to Narnaul or some other town. The village experienced quick rise in its prosperity after the installation of tube wells i.e., in 1975. Due to mechanization of agriculture the production increased many-fold and the economic condition of the farmers improved. A major share of sharply enhanced agriculture incomes was spent on building pucca houses. Many farmers invested considerable share of there incomes on buying agricultural implements such as tractors, trolleys and thrashers and other machinery used for various agricultural operations. Besides, during this period the farmers have improved their standard of living. They purchased coolers, freeze, scooters, washing machines, motorcycles etc.

Another conspicuous consequence of rapid rise in the agriculture incomes due to extension of tube well irrigation was considerable increase in the expenditure on dowry and substantial spurt in the consumption of liquor. Significantly, the expenditure on dowry and liquor has remained virtually as high as that during the peak period of agriculture incomes even after the depletion of ground water and the consequent erosion of agriculture prosperity in the village.

When the village was stricken by acute water scarcity during one and half decade i.e., 1990 to 2005, even drinking water had to be fetched from nearby village Khatoti located at a distance of 2 kilometers nearest Dohan River. The water was either brought on head or on animal carts. During that period the villagers even had to go without bath for days together. It is notable that most of the task of water fetching had to be performed by females. It shows that erosion of resources, including drinking water impacts more adversely on weaker segments of society. The problems of bringing drinking water from another village was solved with the joint efforts of the village panchayat and the Government when a deep tube wells was installed on a small patch of land which was purchased from neighboring village Khatoti Khurd. Mostly all the 90 tube wells of the village are still dry and they are not in operation. The whole cultivated land of the village is rainfed.

With the decline in agricultural incomes after depletion of ground water, the village suffered decline in its social position in the area. Among other one manifestation of its decline social status was that the people from the surrounding villages were not forthcoming to make matrimonial ties in this village. The people did not want to marry their daughters in the village where even drinking water had to be fetched either from adjoining villages or from Narnaul town by tankers. Similarly outside villagers were also not interested in getting brides from

Bhankhri village as not much dowry would be available in context of sustaining poverty among the village population at large. As a result very few marriages took place here during the period of acute water shortage i.e., 1990-95. The people preferred to postpone the marriage in the hope of better days to come. Similarly there was little addition to pucca houses during this period. In the families where there is no person in the secondary or tertiary activities and are fully depended on agriculture they are in very-light position economically.

Conclusion

Introduction of tube well irrigation to semi-arid areas results in notable changes in cropping pattern in favour of cash crops. When the ground water resources get depleted, the cropping pattern reverts more or less to the earlier positions. There occurs a rapid rise and then rapid fall in agricultural incomes with the increase and decrease in area under irrigation. The village also undergoes corresponding enchantment and decline in its social status in the areas. Similarly the scarcity of drinking water resulting from exhaustion of ground water resources by tube well irrigation, further adds to the strain as well as rudgery of female work. Decline in cattle population and even that of trees is another outcome of this situation. It follows from the study that it is not a right approach to apply the method of flood irrigation in semi-arid/arid areas as it is wasteful of scarce ground water resources. To pursue such a practice amount to deliberate undermining of the area as it ultimately exhausts the very foundation of life, i.e., water. Drip irrigation seems to be best suited in such semi-arid condition, besides, water-prudent crops should be grown instead of water expensive crops. Cropping pattern needs to be carefully designed as per the specifications of the local areas. Imitation of cropping pattern of sub-humid and humid tractor that of canal irrigated areas is not a tune with sustainability of semi-arid or arid areas.

In brief, any sustainable development in agriculture could only be achieved in a meaningful manner if it is done after taking into account the socio-economic, culture and ecological pulse of the areas. Any blind duplication of the experience of other areas may do more harm than good to both the land and the people. Water management needs to be accorded a top priority in such areas. So that strengthening of the exciting drought-resistant and drought escaping crops in the study areas might be helpful to a great extent where the scarcity of irrigation is main problem. Various education and training centers should be opened in the study areas to train and educate the farmer about the various rain water harvesting techniques. The Haryana Government should formulate a strategy for ground water recharge. The major trust of the strategy should be to control the depletion of the ground water table through artificial recharge measure and proper water management practice.

References

Dhiya L.N. : Dynamics of Economic life in Rural India, Gain Publishing House New Delhi,1991.

Leaf,M.J. : The Green Revolution and Cultural Changes in a Punjab Village, 1965-78.

Madan G.R. : Changing Pattern of Indian Villages, S.Chand and Co. Delhi, 1969.

Gil, M.S. : Consequences of ground water depletion in semi-arid tract of Haryana.

Yadav, R.N. : The Geographer Vol. 48, No. 2, 2001, pp36-43,AMU, Aligrah.

Smith, W. : Modernization of Traditional Village, Asia Publishing House, Mumbai 1965.

Yadav, R.N. : Changes in Cropping Pattern in Narnaul Tehsil, Ph.D. thesis, Jamia Millia Islamia, New Delhi,1990.

Yadàv, R.N. : Socio-Economic profile of village Nihalgrah, Haryana. A case study. Geographical Review of India Vol.60, No.2, June 1998.

CHAPTER 9

Climate Change and Society: A Global Perspective

DR. M. M. SHEIKH, RAVINDER KUMAR, MRS. BIPIN MANDAR

Lecturer of Geography, Govt. Lohia College, Churu -331 001.

Key words: Global warming, climate change, sea level, soil degradation, crop productivity, hydrological cycle, forest degradation, biodiversity, health, carbon pricing, green tax.

Introduction

Climate is changing at its own pace, since the beginning of evolution of earth but presently it has gained momentum due to inadvertent anthropogenic disturbances. Now a days the question of climate change and its impacts regionally and globally, have moved from the realm of doubts and uncertainties to one of serious concern. Climate change will impact on different regions and sectors differently based on their sensitivities and adaptive capacity and therefore their vulnerability. The most recent statements of the stern review on economics of climate change and intergovernmental panel on climate change (IPCC) bring out convincing evidence of such changes. Climate change can manifest itself in gradual change in sea level, soil fertility, soil erosion, crop productivity, hydrological cycle, water balance, forest degradation, biodiversity and human health etc., resulting in changes in the frequency, intensity and duration of extreme events. Human beings, like other living organisms, have always influenced their environment. It is only since the beginning of the Industrial Revolution, that the impact of human activities has begun to extend to a much larger scale, continental or even global. The impact of human activities now extends to other aspects of climate including ocean warming and rising sea level, continental average temperature, extreme temperature and wind patterns.

Human activities, in particular those involving the combustion of fossil fuels for industrial or domestic usage, and biomass burning, produce greenhouse gases and aerosols which affect the composition of the atmosphere. The emission of chlorofluorocarbons (CFCs) and other chlorine and bromine compounds have not only an impact on the radiative forcing, but have also led to the depletion of the stratospheric ozone layer. Land-use change, due to urbanisation and human forestry and agricultural practices, affect the physical and biological properties of the Earth's surface. Such effects change the radiative forcing and have a potential impact on regional and global climate. About a thousand years before the Industrial Revolution, the amount of greenhouse gases in the atmosphere remained relatively constant. Since then, the concentration of various greenhouse gases has increased. The amount of carbon dioxide, for example, has increased by more than 30 per cent since pre-industrial times and is still increasing at an unprecedented rate of an average 0.4 per cent per year, mainly due to the combustion of fossil fuels and deforestation. The anthropogenic emissions have resulted in a marked increase in atmospheric concentrations of carbon dioxide (CO_2), methane (CH_4) and nitrous oxide (N_2O) since 1750 and now far exceeds "pre-industrialisation" values. The concentration of the nitrogen oxides (NO and NO_2) and of carbon monoxide (CO) are also increasing. Although these gases are not greenhouse gases, they play a role in the atmospheric chemistry and have led to an increase in tropospheric ozone, a greenhouse gas, by 40 per cent since pre-industrial times. The sources are summarized in the figure no. 9.1 given below. The current level or stock of greenhouse gases in the atmosphere is equivalent to around 430 ppm (parts per million) compared with only 280 ppm before the Industrial Revolution. These concentration have already caused the world to warm by more than half a degree Celsius and will lead to at least a further half degree warming over the next few decades, because of the inertia in the climate system. Even if the annual flow of emissions did not increase beyond today's rate, the stock of greenhouse gases in the atmosphere would reach double than pre-industrial levels by 2050 - that is 550 ppm CO_2^e - and would continue growing thereafter. But the annual flow of emissions is accelerating, as fast-growing economies invest in high carbon infrastructure and as demand for energy and transport increases around the world. The level of 550 ppm CO_2^e could be reached as early as 2035. These trends are leading to greater climatic changes.

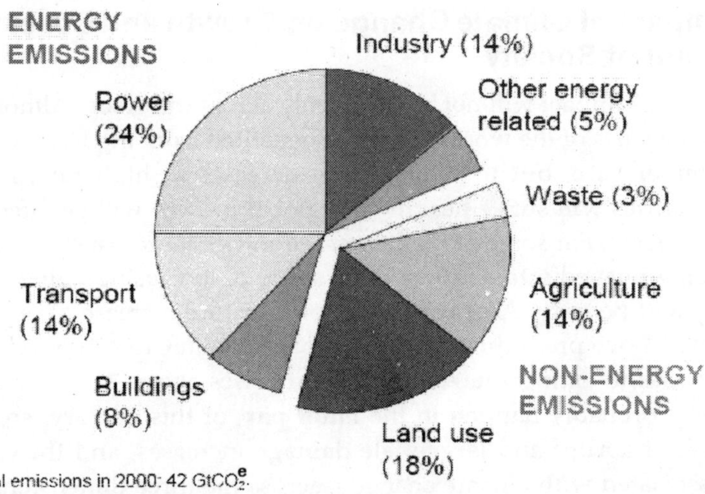

Total emissions in 2000: 42 $GtCO_2^e$.

Energy emissions are mostly CO_2 (some non-CO_2 in industry and other energy related). Non-energy emissions are CO_2 (land-use) and non-CO_2 (agriculture and waste).

Fig. 9.1 : Green house gas emissions in 2000

Climate change is global in its causes and consequences, and international collective action will be critical in driving an effective, efficient and equitable response on the scale required. This response will require deeper international co-operation in many areas - most notably in creating price signals and markets for carbon, spurring technology research, development and deployment, and promoting adaptation, particularly for developing countries. Climate change presents a unique challenge for society. Recently published Stern's report and UN IPCC (Inter–Governmental Panel on Climate Change) report have directly alleged man for climate changes on earth. The size of the ecological footprint is measured according to the rate of over-consumption and exploitation of natural resources, leading to a major impact on society across the globe. It is quite clear now that greenhouse gas emission reductions in the order of sixty to eighty per cent will be needed by the year 2050 to avoid even more drastic climate change. It's a global problem that needs global solutions.

Impact of Climate Change on Growth and Development of Society

The impact will not be felt evenly across the globe. Although some parts of the world would be benefited from modest rises in temperature, but if temperature increases at high rate, most countries will suffer heavily and global growth will be affected adversely. For some of the poorest countries there is a real risk of being pushed into a downwards spiral of increasing vulnerability and poverty. Average global temperature increase of only 1-2°C (above pre-industrial levels) could commit 15-40 per cent of species to extinction. As temperature rises above 2-3°C, as will very probably happen in the latter part of this century, so the risk of abrupt and large-scale damage increases, and the costs associated with climate change – across the three dimensions of mortality, ecosystems and income – are likely to rise more steeply. In mathematical terms, the global damage function is convex. No region would be left untouched by changes of this magnitude, though developing countries would be affected especially adversely. This applies particularly to the poorest people within the large populations of both sub-Saharan Africa, and South Asia. By 2100, in South Asia and Sub-Saharan Africa, up to 145 - 220 million additional people could fall below the $2-a-day poverty line, and every year an additional 165,000 -

250,000 children could die compared with a world without climate change. The review suggests that the risks and costs of climate change over the next two centuries could be equivalent to an average reduction in global per capita consumption of at least 5 per cent, now and forever. The estimated damages would be much higher if non-market impacts the possibility of greater climate sensitivity, and distributional issues were taken into account. The impact on society is estimated through possible effects on water, food, health, land, environment etc.

Water

People will feel the impact of climate change most strongly through changes in the distribution of water around the world and its seasonal and annual variability. Water is an essential resource for all life and a requirement for good health and sanitation. It is a critical input for almost all production and essential for sustainable growth and poverty reduction. The location of water around the world is a critical determinant of livelihood. Globally, around 70 per cent of all freshwater supply is used for irrigating crops and providing food. 22 per cent is used for manufacturing and energy (cooling power stations and producing hydro-electric power), while only 8 per cent is used directly by households and businesses for drinking, sanitation, and recreation. Climate change will alter patterns of water availability by intensifying the water cycle. Droughts and floods will become more severe in many areas. There will be more rain at high latitudes, less rain in the dry subtropics, and uncertain but probably substantial changes in tropical areas. Hotter land surface temperatures induce more powerful evaporation and hence more intense rainfall, with increased risk of flash flooding. Differences in water availability between regions will become increasingly pronounced. Areas that are already relatively dry, such as the Mediterranean basin and parts of Southern Africa and South America, are likely to experience further decreases in water availability, for example, several (but not all) climate models predict upto 30 per cent decrease in annual runoff in these regions for a 2° C global temperature rise and 40-50 per cent for 4°C. In contrast, South Asia and parts of Northern Europe and Russia are likely to experience increases in water availability (runoff), for example, a 10-20 per cent increase for a 2°C temperature, rise and slightly greater increases for 4°C, according to several climate models.

Food

In tropical regions, even small amounts of warming will lead to declines in yield. In higher latitudes, crop yields may increase initially for moderate increases in temperature but then fall. Higher temperatures will lead to substantial declines in cereal production around the world, particularly if the carbon fertilisation effect is smaller than previously thought, as some recent studies suggest. Food production will be particularly sensitive to climate change, because crop yields depend in large part on prevailing climate conditions (temperature and rainfall patterns). Agriculture currently accounts for 24 per cent of world output, employs 22 per cent of the global population, and occupies 40 per cent of the land area. 75 per cent of the poorest people in the world (the one billion people who live on less than $1 a day) live in rural areas and rely on agriculture for their livelihood. Low levels of warming in mid to high latitudes (US, Europe, Australia, Siberia and some parts of China) may improve the conditions for crop growth by extending the growing season and opening up new areas for agriculture. Further warming will have increasingly negative impacts – as temperature thresholds are reached more often and water shortages limit growth in regions such as Southern Europe and Western USA. High temperature episodes can reduce yields by upto half if they coincide with a critical phase in the crop cycle like flowering.

Health

Climate change will increase worldwide deaths from malnutrition and heat stress. Vector-borne diseases such as malaria and dengue fever could become more widespread if effective control measures are not in place. In higher latitudes, cold-related deaths will decrease. Climate-sensitive aspects of human health make up a significant proportion of the global disease burden and may grow in importance. The health of the world's population has improved remarkably over the past 50 years, although striking disparities remain. Slum populations in urban areas are particularly exposed to disease, suffering from poor air quality and heat stress, and with limited access to clean water. In some tropical areas, temperatures may already be at the limit of human tolerance. Peak temperatures in the Indo-Gangetic Plain often already exceed 45°C before the arrival of the monsoon. In contrast, in northern latitudes (Europe, Russia, Canada, United States), global warming may imply overall, fewer deaths because more people are saved from cold-related death in the winter than succumb to heat-related death in the summer. In cities heatwaves will become increasingly dangerous, as regional warming together with the urban heat island effect (where cities concentrate and retain heat) leads to extreme temperatures and more dangerous air pollution incidents. Climate change will amplify health disparities between rich and poor parts of the world. The World Health Organisation (WHO) estimates that climate change since the 1970s is already responsible for over 1.5 million deaths each year through increasing incidence of diarrhoea, malaria and malnutrition, predominantly in Africa and other developing regions. Just a 1°C increase in global temperature above pre-industrial could double annual deaths from climate change to at least 3.0 million according to the WHO. These figures do not account for any reductions in cold-related deaths, which could be substantial. At higher temperatures, death rates will increase sharply, for example, more than millions people are dying from malnutrition each year. Climate change will also affect health via other diseases not included in the WHO modeling.

Land

Sea level rise will increase coastal flooding, raise costs of coastal protection, lead to loss of wetlands and coastal erosion, and increase saltwater intrusion into surface and groundwater. Warming from the last century has already committed the world to rising seas for many centuries to come. Further warming in this century will increase this commitment. Rising sea levels will increase the amount of land lost and people displaced due to permanent inundation, while the costs of sea walls will rise approximately as a square of the required height. Coastal areas are amongst the most densely populated areas in the world and support several important ecosystems on which local communities depend. Critical infrastructure is often concentrated around coastlines, including oil refineries, nuclear power stations, port and industrial facilities. Currently, more than 200 million people live in coastal floodplains around the world, with 2 million Km^2 of land and $1 trillion worth of assets less than 1-m elevation above current sea level. One-quarter of Bangladesh's population (35 million people) lives within the coastal floodplain. Many of the world's major cities (22 of the top 50) are at risk of flooding from coastal surges, including Tokyo, Shanghai, Hong Kong, Mumbai, Kolkata, Karachi, Buenos Aires, St Petersburg, New York, Miami and London. In almost every case, the city relies on costly flood defences for protection. Even if protected, these cities would lie below sea level with a residual risk of flooding like New Orleans today.

Sea level rises will lead to large increases in the number of people whose homes are flooded. According to one study that assumes protection levels rise in line with GDP per capita, between 7-70 million and 20-300 million additional people will be flooded each year by 3 to 4°C of warming causing 20-80 cm of sea level rise (low and high population growth assumptions respectively). 65 Upgrading coastal defences further could partially offset these impacts, but would require substantial capital investment and ongoing maintenance. At higher levels of warming and increased rates of sea level rise, the risks will become increasingly serious. South and East Asia will be most vulnerable because of their large coastal populations in low-lying areas, such as Vietnam, Bangladesh and parts of China

(Shanghai) and India. Millions will also be at risk around the coastline of Africa, particularly in the Nile Delta and along the west coast. Small island states in the Caribbean, and in the Indian and Pacific Oceans (e.g., Micronesia and French Polynesia, the Maldives, Tuvalu) are acutely threatened, because of their high concentrations of development along the coast. In the Caribbean, more than half the population lives within 1.5 Km of the shoreline.

Some estimates suggest that 150 - 200 million people may become permanently displaced by the middle of the century due to rising sea levels, more frequent floods, and more intense droughts. Climate change could lead to as many as 150 - 200 million environmental refugees by the middle of the century (2 per cent of projected population). Climate change will lead to hundreds of millions more people without sufficient water or food to survive or threatened by dangerous floods and increased disease. People may also be driven to migrate within a region. A possible climate-induced shift in population and economic activity from southern regions to northern regions of Europe and the USA. Increased storm intensity could cause similar impacts and will exacerbate the effects of sea level rise.

Environment

Climate change is likely to occur too rapidly for many species to adapt. One study estimates that around 15-40 per cent of species face extinction with 2°C of warming. Strong drying over the Amazon, as predicted by some climate models, would result in dieback of forest with the highest biodiversity on the planet. The warming of the 20th century has already directly affected ecosystems. Over the past 40 years, species have been moving pole wards by 6 Km. on average per decade, and seasonal events, such as flowering or egg-laying, have been occurring several days earlier each decade. Coral bleaching has become increasingly prevalent since the 1980s. Arctic and mountain ecosystems are acutely vulnerable – polar bears, caribou and white spruce have all experienced recent declines.

Climate change has already contributed to the extinction of over 1 per cent of the world's amphibian species from tropical mountains. Ecosystems will be highly sensitive to climate change. For many species, the rate of warming will be too rapid to withstand. Many species will have to migrate across fragmented landscapes to stay within their "climate envelope" (at rates that many will not be able to achieve). Migration becomes more difficult with faster rates of warming. In some cases, the "climate envelope" of a species may move beyond reach, for example, moving above the tops of mountains or beyond coastlines. Conservation reserves may find their local climates becoming less amenable to the native species. Other pressures from human activities, including land-use change, harvesting/hunting, pollution and transport of alien species around the world, have already had a dramatic effect on species and will make it even harder for species to cope with further warming. Since 1500, 245 extinctions have been recorded across most major species groups, including mammals, birds, reptiles, amphibians, and trees. A further 800 known species in these groups are threatened with extinction. A warming world will accelerate species extinctions and has the potential to lead to the irreversible loss of many species around the world, with most kinds of animals and plants affected. Rising levels of carbon dioxide have some direct impacts on ecosystems and biodiversity, but increases in temperature and changes in rainfall will have even more profound effects. Vulnerable ecosystems are likely to disappear almost completely at even quite moderate levels of warming. The Arctic will be particularly hard hit, since many of its species, including polar bears and seals, will be very sensitive to the rapid warming predicted and substantial loss of sea ice.

Suggestions

1. The impacts of climate change has the potential to seriously damage the world economy. Recently released Stern report forecasts that world needs to spend one per cent of GDP –

equivalent to about £ 184 bn – dealing with climate change now, or face a bill between 05 and 20 times higher for damage caused by retting it continue. Unchecked climate change could thus cost as much as £ 566 for every man, woman and child now on the planet – roughly 6.5 billion people. What the world urgently needs is "global compact" to fight climate change.

2. The two mechanism for addressing climate change are mitigation and adaption. Mitigation refers to efforts to prevent further climate change. It involves technical and policy measures to reduce the emission of greenhouse gases and stabilize their concentration in the atmosphere. Adaption is adjustment in natural or human systems in response to actual or expected climate change. Policy to reduce emissions should be based on three essential elements: carbon pricing, technology policy, and removal of barriers to behavioural change. Establishing a carbon price, through tax, trading or regulation, is an essential foundation for climate-change policy. Policies are required to support the development of a range of low-carbon and high-efficiency technologies on an urgent timescale. The removal of barriers to behavioural change is a third essential element, one that is particularly important in encouraging the take-up of opportunities for energy efficiency. An effective response to climate change will depend on creating the conditions for international collective action which needs following policy measures:

(*i*) Creating a broadly similar carbon price signal around the world, and using carbon finance to accelerate action in developing countries, are urgent priorities for international co-operation.

(*ii*) Adaptation policy is crucial for dealing with the unavoidable impacts of climate change, but it has been under-emphasised in many countries.

(*iii*) Scaling up flows of carbon finance to developing countries to support effective policies and programmes for reducing emissions would accelerate the transition to a low-carbon economy.

(*iv*) Building and sustaining collective action is now an urgent challenge. Greater international co-operation to accelerate technological innovation and diffusion will reduce the costs of mitigation.

(*v*) Curbing deforestation is a highly cost-effective way of reducing greenhouse gas emissions.

(*vi*) Adaptation efforts in developing countries must be accelerated and supported, including through international development assistance.

(*vii*) More green taxes including 'a global warming premium' on exotic fruit, vegetables and flowers flown thousands of miles across the world.

References

Fankhauser, S. and Tol, R.S.J. (2003): 'On climate change and economic growth', Resource and Energy Economics.

Gedney, N., Cox, P.M. and Huntingford, C. (2004): 'Climate feedback from wetland methane emissions', Geophysical Research Letters.

Hitz, S. and Smith, J.B. (2004): 'Estimating global impacts from climate change', The Benefits of Climate Change Policies.

Hope, C. (2005): 'Integrated assessment models' in Helm, D. (ed.), Climate-change policy, Oxford: Oxford University Press.

Intergovernmental Panel on Climate Change (2001): The Scientific Basis. Contribution of Working Group I to the Third Assessment Report of the Intergovernmental Panel on Climate Change [Houghton JT, Ding Y, Griggs DJ *et al.* (Eds.)], Cambridge: Cambridge University Press.

Smith, J.B. *et al.* (2001): 'Vulnerability to climate change and reasons for concern: a synthesis' Climate Change 2001: Impacts, Adaptation and Vulnerability, Intergovernmental Panel on Climate Change. Cambridge: Cambridge University Press.

Stern Review Report: The Economics of Climate Change.

CHAPTER 10

Degradation of Natural Vegetation is a Big Hazard in Shekhawati Region-Rajasthan

DR. RAJENDRA ACHRA

Lecturer, Deptt. of Geography, Vinodini P.G.College, Khetri (Jhunjhunu).

Introduction

"Natural vegetation is considered to be the best expression of the totality of the climate" – Koppen. From a long time it has been felt by the society of environmental conservation welfare people in the world that natural vegetation should be protected, preserved, and reserved at any cost to save the future of the next generation, not an individual but at global level. It has been resolved and decided after several meeting on environmental conservation at global level, portfolio and policies were formulated for implementation of the management of green coverage specially the forest resources that each and every country or a geographical region should have at least 33% or more than that of total area under forest cover. In other words to say "one-third land-use of any country or region should be under the title of forest land-use".

In this way, the similar efforts have been carried out by each country, state, region and district to enhance the land under green coverage, in this direction. Afforestation and plantation programmes have been implemented by the public as well as private sector. People's participation has been realised several times for the implementation of the forest policies and for the enhancement of the green coverage in that particular area. It is quite obvious in the eyes of environmentalists that sustainable development of a particular area is possible with the enhancement of green coverage, hence the Forest Department in public sector and NGOs in private sector are making their efforts for some decades in this direction. Specially afforestation programmes have been carried out time to time by the Department of Forest, Aravalli project and Social Forestry.

In scientific perception, "a forest is that area which is closed with a boundary, dense vegetation and more percentage of trees." All kind of efforts are made either from public or from private sector - the ultimate target is to enhance the land under forest as well as vegetation coverage. Further in this context, there are two kinds of forest areas—State forest sector and private forest areas i.e. from private sector. State forest is further classified into three - Reserve forest, Protected forest, and Unclassed forest whereas private forest is also further classified into two categories area of closed under Indian Forest Act. In this way total forest area of the district includes both kind of forest i.e., State Forest and Private Forest.

Reduction in natural vegetation is mainly a man-made problem, resulting from excessive degradation of natural vegetation viz., trees, herbs, shrubs, under shrubs, grasses and climbers under any ecosystem or habitat. By thus, the problem of decreasing natural vegetation is a continuous one because of increasing biotic interferences but it could be controlled to a great extent by improved forest management practices.

Study Area

Shekhawati region is located in the north-eastern part of Rajasthan state and the region has geographical extension from 26°26′ to 29°20′ north latitude and 74°44′ to 76°34′ east longitude on the map of Rajasthan. The area under study covers fully or partly three districts, namely Churu, Jhunjhunu and Sikar. Churu district's out of 7, only 3 tehsils fall under Shekhawati region (Churu, Rajgarh and Taranagar) whereas Jhunjhunu district as a whole with its six tehsils (Buhana, Chirawa, Khetri,

Jhunjhunu, Nawalgarh and Udaipurwati) in which Buhana tehsil emerged out as a new tehsil on the map of Jhunjhunu district (2001), it was no where in existence in the year of 1991 and Sikar district also covered fully with its six tehsils (Data Ramgarh, Fatehpur, Laxmangarh, Neem ka Thana, Sikar and Shri Madhopur). The region has 23 Panchayat Samitis in all. Thus, the region under study has 15 tehsils in total with its total 15343 sq. km geographical area which makes 5.6% of the state's total. At the part of district-wise contribution by area point of view in Shekhawati region it is observed that part and portion of Churu district contributes 29%, Jhunjhunu district contributes 31% and Sikar by 40%, respectively. Among these tehsils area point of view, the tehsil of Churu is largest one and Buhana smallest, respectively. According to the District-wise area, Sikar stands at first position which is followed by Jhunjhunu and lowest contribution is made by Churu i.e., 1683 sq. km only.

Methodology

The present study has been substantiated by extensive field work. The essential data have been collected from a wide range of sources. The remote sensing available data have been used. Survey of India topo-sheets for the entire region and a bioclimatic map have been used as base maps. Additionally, data from reports, maps, pamphlets, research papers, books, monographs, soil survey data, forest survey data from published and unpublished materials have been collected from different agencies. After examining the remote sensing and other data related to physical (climate, soil, land forms and water), biological (flora and fauna) and social (population dynamics, economic activities, land-use and productivity) indicators, a few survey sites were located. The sites were visited during field survey.

Changing Aspect in Natural Vegetation

Distribution of 'forest cover' point of view in the area under study, one can be divided into two obvious parts : first, Non-

Forest Area and second, Forest Area which is mostly Open Forest by having 'crowd density' 10 to 40 per cent. By thus, it covers-protected forest area, preserve as well as reserve forest area. According to the statistical analysis of 1991, the Shekhawati region covered 13.44% of the total forest area of its three districts' total geographical area which was 2.95 per cent of the states total area under forest in which Sikar ranked at first (7.35%), Jhunjhunu at second (5.91%) and Churu at third (0.21%).

Table 10.0 : Forest Coverage/Area in Shekhawati Region, Rajasthan

Name of the District	*Forest Area (In %)*		*Changing in Forest Area (In %)*
	1991	*2001*	
Jhunjhunu	5.91	6.84	0.93
Sikar	7.35	8.27	0.92
Churu	0.21	0.47	0.26
Shekhawati Region (% Contribution in Rajasthan)	13.44 (2.95)	15.58 (3.46)	+ 2.14 (0.51)

Source : Resource Atlas of Rajasthan, Jaipur

It is mentioned in above Table 10.0 in 2001, the forest coverage/area enhanced about 2.14% and thus the area under forest reaches to 15.58% of total forest area of three districts, total geographical area which makes 3.46% per cent of the states total area under forest in which again Sikar ranks at first place (8.27%), followed by Jhunjhunu (6.84%) and lowest by Churu (0.47%). It is interesting to mention here that among all three districts of Shekhawati region, the maximum forest coverage enhancement took place in Sikar (8.27%) and lowest by Churu (0.47%). It is really very interesting to mention here that among all three districts of Shekhawati region, the maximum forest coverage/area enhancement (0.93%) took place in Jhunjhunu district during the course of last one decade i.e., 1991 to 2001.

It is a very surprising finding on the basis of available data records, the percentage area of land under forest in Rajasthan State gradually increasing but the forest area under Shekhawati Region is gradually decreasing. Table 10.1 obviously illustrates that it is a matter to think all of us, specially the environmentalists, forest department, botanists and concerning authorities that overall in Rajasthan state the rate of per annum although very low i.e., 0.004 but towards development is a good symbol of greenery enhancement whereas in Shekhawati region the rate of per annum is about seven times high (0.51%) from the state i.e., -0.35 but towards shrinkage which is a bad symbol of alarming status of greenery declination.

Table 10.1 : Change Detection of Vegetation Status

S. No.	*Vegetation Status*	*Area (in percentage)*		*Change Detection (in %)*
		July,1990	*July,2002*	
1.	Very High	1.7	-	-1.7
2.	High	8.4	5.0	-3.4
3.	Moderate	7.3	8.3	+1
4.	Low	27.3	24.7	-2.6
5.	Poor	30.4	49.0	+18.6
6.	Very Poor	24.9	13.0	-11.9
	Total	100	100	

Source : Based on NOVA data analysis

Status of Green Coverage in 1990

Table 10.0 is the presentation of green coverage of Shekhawati region on the basis of Satellite imagery interpretation of July 1990 as supplied by RRSSC, Jodhpur which naturally illustrates the distribution of the green coverage on that time and duration.

As per vegetation status, it is very interesting to mention here that the region during 1990 has a category of "very high vegetation status" which covers only 1.7 per cent in Table 10.1. The "poor vegetation status category" covers maximum percentage from area point of view i.e., 30.4 per cent and it is followed by "low category of vegetation status". The area like barren land indicated as "very poor category of vegetation status" covers about 25 per cent. The area also covers 8.4 per cent "high category of vegetation status" which is followed by "moderate category of vegetation status" by covering 7.3 per cent. Very high, high and moderate categories of vegetation status overall make about 18 per cent of the region under study which is not so far more satisfactory position from green coverage point of view.

Status of Green Coverage in 2002

Table 10.1 is the presentation of green coverage of Shekhawati region on the basis of satellite imagery of the same month i.e., July of 2002 as supplied by RRSSC, Jodhpur which naturally shows the distribution of green coverage on the areas of dense vegetation as well as forest sites and open vegetation sites on during that period i.e., 2002.

It is mentioned in Table 10.1, the region under study has five categories of vegetation status in which the maximum percentage is covered by "poor category of vegetation status" i.e., 49.0 per cent. The "category of vegetation status" has only 5.0 per cent coverage in the region which is followed by "moderate category of vegetation status" by covering 8.3 per cent respectively. "Low category of vegetation status" makes high percentage of the area under study i.e., 24.7 per cent whereas "very poor category of vegetation status" which is like barren land covers about 13 per cent.

Change Detection in Status of Green Coverage

The forthcoming paragraphs of this research paper deals with the interpretation of the status of green coverage in Shekhawati region on the basis of two Satellite Imageries supplied by RRSSC - Jodhpur, Rajasthan. The Table 10.1 deals with the geographical distribution of vegetation cover during 1990 and 2002, the table illustrates region-wise data of the percentage of geographical areas of the villages land which fall under the Dense forest, Open forest and Dense vegetation which also emphasises to some extent the contribution of the efforts made by Departments of Forest, Shekhawati region, Rajasthan.

It is very interesting to mention here that development in the categories of "moderate" (+ 1.0%) and "poor" vegetation status took place during last twelve years as shown in Table 10.1. It is matter of bad symbol that disappearance of "very high" and "high" category of vegetation status took place by (-1.7% and -3.4%) for the region under study. "Low" category of vegetation status also decreases by –2.6% during the course of last twelve years. In this way the Table 10.1. illustrates the assessment of change detection of vegetation status in Shekhawati region, Rajasthan, respectively.

Conclusion

Natural vegetation degradation is taking place in Shekhawati region through irregular rainfall, public interfere, wind erosion, water erosion, high temperature, storms and soil erosion. These processes have been accelerated by increasing technological and human activities it has resulted in the degradation of natural vegetation of the region due to irregular rainfall and wind erosion and high temperature are more serious and widespread. Overgrazing and indiscriminate falling of trees resulted in the degradation of vegetation cover and decrease in biomass production. In case these problems continue uncontrolled, large acreage of forest area will be affected in future. By thus, the decrease in natural vegetation in Shekhawati region is a bad symbol of environmental degradation which naturally plays role as a speed barrier in the sustainable development of the region under study in future.

References

Anonymous, 1991 : Nature and Extent of Biodiversity in Arid and Semi-arid Region of India, CAZRI Jodhpur.

Bachketi, N.D. 1984 : Social Forestry in India, Problems and Prospects, Published by Birla Institute of Scientific Research, New Delhi.

Bhandari M.M. 1990 : Flora of the Indian Desert (Revised) MPS Report Jodhpur.

Cain, S.A. and Castro, G.M.de O., 1959 : Manual of Vegetation Analysis. Arper and Row, U.S.A.

Clements, F.E. 1916 : Plants succession - An analysis of the development of vegetation. Washington, D.C.

Eyre, S.R. 1963 : Vegetation and Soils : A World Picture, Edward Arhold.

Hills, E.S. 1966 : (ed.), Arid Lands, UNESCO and Methuen.

Hooker, J.D. 1906. A Sketch of the flora of British India, London.

Koppen, W.P. 1900 : Versuch einer Klassification for Klimate, uorzugsweise nachihren beziehurgen zur planzenwett. Geogr. Z. 6:593-611.

Krebs, C.J. 1978 : Ecology - The Experimental Analysis of distribution and abundance. Harper and Raw.

Levin, D.A. 1979 : The nature of plant species, Sci 204. 381-4.

Linneaus, S.C. 1753 : Species Plantarum.

Mani, M.S. 1974 : Ecology and Biogeography in India. Dr. W. Junk. B.V. Publishers, The Hague.

Money, D.C. 1965 : Climate, Soil and Vegetation. University of Tutorial Press, U.K.

Sharma, M.K. 2007 : Medical Plant Geography, Rachana Publications, Jaipur.

Polunin, 1967 : Introducing of Plant Geography and some related Science. London.

Rathore, N.S. 1992 : Application of Remote Sensing in Forest Cover Mapping of North Aravalli's Mountains Ranges. XIV-Indian Geography Congress, Jaipur, Abstract Publication, pp. - 31.

Raunkiaer, C. 1934 : The Life-forms of the plant and statistical plant geography. Clarendon Press. Oxford.

Robinson, H. 1978 : Biogeography. MacDonald and Evan, London.

Shankar, V. and Kumar, S. 1988 : Vegetation ecology of the Indian Thar desert. International Journal of Ecology Environmental Sciences 14: 131-155.

Shivshwami, N. and Shriniwasan, V. 1977 : The role of trees in the control of environmental pollution. Expl. News : 21(52) pp- 52, New Delhi.

Vietmeyer, N.D. 1986 : Lesser-known Plant of Potential use in Agricultural and Forestry Sci., 232, 1379-84.

Watts, D. 1971 : Principles of Biogeography. McGraw Hill, London.

Wegner, P.L. 1965 : Vegetation and Soils. Mc Graw Hill, New York.

World Resource Institute, 1992 : World Resources. Oxford University Press, New York.

CHAPTER 11

Application of Remote Sensing and GIS to Water Resources Management

DR. B. C. JAT

Lecturer of Geography, Govt. P.G. College, Neem ka Thana, Rajasthan.

Introduction

The practice of hydrology has become increasing computational during the past several years. The advanced development in computers has provided an important tool to the decision-makers for carrying out hydrology analysis for water resources planning and development. The soil and water are of crucial importance for mankind and these are nature's gift to us. The continuing and accelerating depletion created many problems, deforestation, faulty cultivation, overgrazing, changing life style and increased pressure of urban population on land. Thus, continuous degradation of production base and imbalance in land-water-plant-human-animal system is leading to ecological imbalance and economic insecurity through severe soil erosion.

It is estimated (Das, 1985), that out of total reported geographical area 329 million hectares, about 167 mha (51% of the total area) are affected by serious problems of which 127 mha are affected to serious soil erosion and 40 mha area degraded are through gullies and ravines, shifting, cultivation, water logging, salinity, alkalinity etc., in a recent analysis of annual soil erosion rate in India (Dhurva Narayan and Ram Babu, 1983). It was estimated that about 53 million tonnes (16.35 tonnes/ha) of soil is detached annually due to agriculture and associated activities alone. The country's rivers carry about 2052 million tonnes (6026 tonnes/ha), of this and nearly 1572 million tonnes (29% of the total eroded soil), are carried away by the river into the sea every year and 480 million tonnes (10% of the total eroded soil) are being deposited in various reservoirs resulting in considerable loss of the storage capacity.

Therefore, at present time the most attention is being given on soil erosion problem. The development of recent technologies e.g. Remote Sensing and Geographical Information System are very useful for management of soil and water resources. Scientific management of soil and water resources on watershed basis is therefore very important to arrest rapid soil erosion. Watershed basis scientific management require a good database of watershed such as watershed boundary, drainage map, various watershed characteristics, accurate and reliable observed runoff and sediment yield data. Satellite Remote Sensing provides us scientific input for formulation of appropriate watershed management programs and parameters related to watershed development. Many parametric method has been developed to estimate soil erosion. The most commonly used method for estimation of soil erosion is Universal Soil Loss Equation (USLE) presented by Wishmeier (1959) in USA. This equation can be modeled in geographical information system environment. Various factors can be determined by using Remote Sensing and GIS. In this research work maps we got the priority class of each sub-watersheds after crossing land-use/land cover map, Hydrologic soil group map and classified slope map.

A Geographical Information System is a specific information system applied to geographical data and is mainly referred for as system of hardware, software and procedure designed to support the capture management, manipulation, analyzing, modeling and display of spatially referred date for solving complex planning and management problems. Geographical Information System links land cover data to topographical data and to other information concerning processes and properties related to geographical location when applied to hydrologic system. Hydrologic application of GIS has ranged from synthesis and characterization of hydrologic tendencies to prediction of response of hydrologic events i.e. Rainfall-Runoff modeling.

Surface Water Inventory and Surveying

Due to the strong contrast between water and surrounding surfaces afforded by satellite near infra-red observations, surface water becomes the most easily delineable parameter in the hydrologic cycle. This satellite ability to map surface water is thus very exciting because it permits the rapid inventorying of water bodies over a large geographic region. In the infra-red electromagnetic wavelength, incident radiation is absorbed by water whereas surrounding land and vegetation reflects. Because of this phenomenon, surface water appears black on reflective infra-red images.

With the type of satellite derived surface coverage information, over a period of time inventory can be made either river basin-wise or for a district/state, as to:

- Location
- Numbers
- Areal extent
- Periodic fluctuation
- Water quality status (turbid *vs* clear water)
- Water quantity status (shallow *vs* deep water)

This may help in planning likely utilization potential in terms of:

- Agricultural water supply
- Drinking water supply
- Possible source of recharge to groundwater aquifer.

Such tank inventory entirely by conventional means is time consuming, constantly and impractical.

Hydrologic Studies

Due to shortage of observed hydrologic data, it is very

much essential to utilise the available data in developing a relationship between the input data i.e. rainfall, which can be utilized subsequently to estimate required hydrologic parameters in rainfall-runoff modeling, water balance studies, runoff forecasting. The data required are mostly accurate and reliable hydrologic data (runoff data, evaporation data, meteorological data), satellite acquired during same season/period of observed hydrological data and of course a suitable hydrologic model to take input from the observed data and satellite data.

Watershed Conservation Planning and Management

Problems associated with soil erosion, movement and deposition of sediment in rivers, lakes and estuaries persist though the geologic ages in almost all parts of the earth; but the situation is more aggravated in recent times with humankind's increasing intervention with the environment. "Transformation of virgin lands into agricultural use and faulty agricultural practices, mismanagement and development words". The resulting situation is loss of soil's productivity, drought, flood, silitation in reservoir, poor goundwater recharge and finally further deterioration of our fragile environment.

Scientific management of soil, water and vegetation resources on watershed basis is, therefore, very important to arrest rapid siltation in rivers, lakes and estuaries. Watershed basis scientific management required a good database of the watershed such as watershed boundary, drainage map, various watershed characteristics, accurate and reliable observed runoff and sediment yield data. Inspite of availability of all these data, it is, however, realized that due to financial and organizational constraints, it is not feasible to treat the entire watershed within a short time. Prioritizing of watersheds on the basis of those sub-watersheds within a watershed which contribute maximum sediment yield obviously should determine our priority to evolve appropriate conservation management strategy so that maximum benefit can be derived out of any such money time effort making scheme.

Flood Plan Management

Flood damage surveys are essential not only to assess the extent and severity of damage caused by the floods periodically in river valleys but also for economic evaluation of flood control measures. Moreover, timeliness of information is crucial for managing events like flood. Remote sensing admirably facilitates flood survey by providing much needed information on flood inundated areas and flood damage assessment, flood-plain land use and soil and certain natural flood susceptibility indicators are helpful. Such information from multi-date satellite data on spatial and temporal domains can be derived in cost and time effective means.

In India, mapping flood affected area using satellite data is quite developed at present regarding time and cost effectiveness using satellite data, time factor to prepare a flood inundation map using image interpretation technique at a Remote Sensing Work Centre in India will be around 10 days from the date of acquisition of satellite data. If IRS-1A/Landsat TM image FCC is used, cost of such mapping is expected to be of the order of 12 paisa per sq. km. (Central Water Commission, 1990).

In 1988 flood season, near real-time flood mapping and assessment of crop damages due to floods in Ganga and Brahmaputra basins were carried out by the National Remote Sensing Agency. Comparison of crop area damaged during 1988 by Brahmaputra floods in Assam as estimated from satellite images and as per conventional flood damage reporting reveals that the former gives 33 per cent less estimated crop damage acreage than the later one.

Flood affected and crop damage in lower reach of Kosi flood-plain was monitored using multi-date satellite data of 1988 with respect to rise in river flood leveler. Their relationship was then utilized to anticipate flood affected area of 1989 flood season. Difference between anticipated and actual (from satellite imagery of 1989) was close to 8.3% denitrification and mapping of flood-prone areas are necessary for proper land-use planning for flood-prone area owing to keep flood damage to the minimum. Flood events of various magnitudes and recurrence intervals in the historic past might have left certain flood susceptibility indicators which are helpful in delineation of flood-prone areas. Factors to take into account broadly include meteorologic, physiographic, topographic, geomorphic, pedologic and land-use. Remote sensing data provide significant information in later three factors.

Water Management in Irrigation Command Areas

Multi-spectral and multi-temporal remote sensing provides significant informational crop type discrimination, crop acreage estimation, and irrigation source-wise cropland identification through image interpretation, digital classification and change detection techniques. Identifying irrigated croplands are relatively easier in FCC image from most land resources satellite/ sensor (IRS-LISS III/Landsat TM) because of associated irrigated water sources (Canal/tank/river-lift) information.

Monitoring the status of crop acreage and irrigation water requirement vis-a-vis irrigation water supplies is important to obtain a realistic view of the "irrigation potential" and "potential utilized" Satellite data provides most useful source of area-wise crop estimation and net irrigation water requirements, and the quantity of irrigation supply and efficiency in application.

- In the context need for judicious management of our limited water resources, basic hydrologic data and monitoring are required. Remote sensing has many advantages vis-a-vis conventional hydrologic surveys to meet some of these requirements.
- Technology suitable for satellite based water resources assessment is outlined in this paper, with special emphasis on currently available satellite remote sensing data over India.

- Greatest strength of satellite remote sensing is its ability to identify, measure, map inventory, monitor, model, forecast, surveillance of hydrologic events and phenomena. While many of these are in operational and semi-operational mode, remote sensing activities ahead of us held better promise for space hydrology.
- While it may well be appreciated that not all elements of 'water cycle' are amenable to remote sensing. Remote sensing can aid in some of the water resources development programs, if judiciously applied and understood.
- Building up of trained manpower on the one hand and case studies and practical problem solving on the other hand in this emerging technology is the need of the hour for the water resources planning agencies in the country to derive maximum benefit of hardware being put into space and the advantages offered by satellite hydrology.

References

Aggarwal, S.P. (1999) : Water resources issues and consequences for data and planning. Water resources division. IIRS Dehradun PP1-6.

Abrahm, Thomas, Sharma, P.K., Sharma, M.K. and Sood, A. (1999) : Hydrogeomorphological mapping assessing groundwater by using remote sensing data, A case study in lower Ganga block, Sangrur district, Punjab. Journal of the Indian society of remote sensing vol. 27 No. 1 pp 31-42.

Jat, B.C. (1999) : Watershed prioritization and Rainfall modeling of bandal watershed : A remote sensing and GIS Approach, submitted to WRD. Indian Institute of Remote Sensing Dehradun.

Lillesand, T.M. and Kiefer, R.W. (1994) : Remote Sensing and Image Interpretation. John Wiley & sons. New York pp 202-213.

Water resources division (1999) : Later notes on GIS Applications in water resource management. Indian Institute of Remote Sensing pp 1-5.

CHAPTER 12

Role of Vegetation - Agro System to Check Natural Hazards in the Mountains

S. K. BANDOONI AND JAGAT SINGH CHAUDHARY "JUNGLEE"

Introduction

There is a rapid increase in natural disasters in the mountains of Himalaya due to increase in population, a scientific exploitation, lack of proper management etc. The problems of heavy rainfall and landslide have been arising due to changing weather. Whereas the preserved snow of Himalaya has been melting rapidly. Water level of rivers, which originates from Himalaya is increasing day by day. Expansion in hilly farming without tree plantation causes speedy soil loss. Loss of forests and bio-diversity have made the farming land un-fertile and public life is terribly disturbed because of water logging and flood in rivers, canals, etc.

The amount of water resources is getting decreased because of lack of rain. Awesome fire in pine and monoculture forest has brought the atmosphere at low level. Violent wild animals are creating danger for human being by entering their houses and lack of concern, for environment has increased the greediness of humans, consequently unlimited exploitation of natural resources are giving height to natural disasters.

The Himalayan sensitive regions including forestland, vegetation, water, soil, wild animals, etc. all are interconnected with each other in natural environment. Since many people living in the Himalayan region are intimated attached with these, but today, the ecological system of Himalaya is going to be imbalanced. The need of hour is to keep it balanced and it can only be horrible if we develop an overall vegetation-agro or mixed forest farming there.

The theme of present paper is to convey the message for developing vegetation-agro farming, which has been successfully implemented by an individual effort with the help of micro biotechnology using the personal and community land, which was barren earlier and the soil erosion was taking place and the danger of landsliding was looming at large. After the intensive work of about 25 years, it has 60 species of trees used for fodder, fuel, furniture wood, fruits, oils and medicinal purposes, 20 types of flora which remain green throughout the year, cash crops such as turmeric, ginger, cardamom, pulses, creepers and seasonal vegetables, tea, beetles, flower, etc.

Under this farming, having used the dug-hole technology successfully to increase the fertility by utilizing plant manure and to solve water problems by producing root canals to mixed-forest farming. By preserving moisture after growing vegetation in barren altitude plants above 1500 mts from sea level. Having taken preventive measures from soil erosion and fire fighting calamity such as landslide and flood have been controlled successfully. Having developed the right-technology for land-use and developing the diversity and plants without any harm it has given new dimensions to economy.

Therefore, there is a need to promote all round development of vegetation-agro farming in the Himalayan region to reduce the tendency of human greed, which disturb the natural processes e.g. landslides and floods elsewhere.

Study Area

Uttaranchal, standing almost, centrally in the Himalaya is also known as the 'Garh-kum region'. The eastern part of it is dominated by Kumauni culture, whereas the western part is dominated by Garhwali culture. The Garhwallies between 29^0 26' N lat-31^0 28' N lat and 78^0 49' E long - 80^0 06' E long with a total area of 29,089 sqm. It is bounded by Tibet (China) in the north, Kumaun in the east, Uttar Pradesh in the south and Himachal Pradesh in the west. Administratively, the region embraces Uttarkashi, Chamoli, Rudraprayag, Tehri, Dehradun and Pauri district and these are divided into 49 Development Blocks for planning. The Rudraprayag is the smallest district in the whole Garhwal. Northern part of the district has the Greater Himalaya, while the southern part has hills and valleys of Lesser Himalaya. Kot Malla village is situated in the one ridge of Haryali ka danda of Lesser Himalaya and having the warm temperate climate. This village is famous for the development of vegetation-agro system under the guidance of one of the author of the present paper (Mr. Jagat Singh Chaudhary).

Experiences

The Himalaya is of great significance to the world. Around 60 per cent of world population is directly or indirectly dependent on Himalayan region. Here nature has endowed man with good opportunities. The Himalaya has influenced the monsoon and lifestyle of northern (China etc.) and southern (India etc.) countries. Due to the origin of various rivers, from Himalaya, most of the population is mainly dependant on agriculture. It is making possible to feed number of people of this region.

India is also a country, which is highly influenced by the Himalayan range of mountains. The Himalaya is also famous for high cultural values. The great cultural conception/value of "Vasudev Kutumbnkum" [i.e. the whole world is one family] had also been originated here. Indian culture representing the concept of " Global Village" which is nothing but to follow the path suggested by an old age perception the "Vasudev Kutumbnkum".

In Himalayan region, the farming has already been dependant, on forests since long back. The forests are helpful in construction works, herbs, wild fruits and vegetables, and good quality dung fertilizer that's obtained from the dry leaves laid in cattle homes. The life in the Himalaya region is self dependant as the origin of many rivers are the source of water. But growing population, expansion of forest, reduction in the number of water sources, the difficulty faced by women while collecting fodder, growing problem of fuel, loss of human life by wild animals, drought due to change in weather, irregular nature of rainfall and snowfall and landslide due to heavy rains; natural crisis like flood, and water-crisis are making the village economy dependant on the market economy. It cannot be called as sustainable. The fleeing unemployments and unplanned developments have made the problem more serious. The vegetation-agro or mixed forest can be a solution of the problem, the utilization of unused empty land between tree to tree, without causing any soil erosion could be minimized and be made more fertile and it could also be ensured that the soil is firm against through mixed forest and cultivation. The financial benefit can also be achieved by growing ginger, turmeric, cardamom, green fodder, pulses, roots, vegetables and flowers in between the trees. The main theme of this paper is to convey the individual's effort that are made in mixed forest farming. With this problem of landslide, on the other hand ecological balance can also be maintained.

Being a farmer the work of vegetation-agro farming is based on Scrobitechnology. Thirty years back this land was barren in which small bushy trees of oak and pines were there. Protecting them by so tonical fencing, trees of fodder and fuel races were afforested. Plants were grown by sowing seeds of oak, bheemal, khari, timla, khaina, chhandra, kachnar sadan, rowania, aakeceia, manipuribanj, chamkharik, pines petrola, kail, devdar, bans, sagam rinigal, tugala, etc. here and there. When a forest of mixed races was ready, the vacant space was used in such a way that could stop soil erosion by lowering water flow. The rainwater was absorbed in the soil inspite of flowing uselessly.

With this it got success in preventing landslide, the heavy and rapid runoff and flow of soil stones. Roots of trees of mixed species made the land firm whereas, by growing ginger, turmeric, cardamom, vegetables, evergreen grasses, feather leaves and flowers in unused land created new dimensions for the economy as well. In the beginning water was fetched through vessels from 2 km away and help of all the family members was sought. Botanical fencing of Ramvans, nag fhani, sinwali, karona, kunja was added to protect vegetation-agro farming from cattles and wild animals.

Vegetation-agro farming has many direct as well as indirect benefits. Landslides can be prevented through this. Due to different shapes and nature of mixed species they make a ring beneath the earth so that grip of earth becomes strong, growing of cash crops is not only beneficial financially but also strengthens the upper layer of earth. By growing perennial grass, mainly napier, kakaoot, joitstar, tachhula, kagaulaya, telia, etc. whose roots grip the earth strongly, problem of fodder-collecting women has also been solved.

Initially there would be difficulty, as people may not be interested in barren land. Due to lack of resources the people are shifting to the cities. Mr. Jagat Singh Chaudhary was also of the same opinion. His wife was also insisting me to get some job in the city. Same was the opinion of the local people. They said nothing would come out from these barren lands. But the aunt of Mr. Jagat Singh Chaudhary, Mrs. Sita Devi was the only lady who inspired me to think about it. Today because of all this, the benefits of vegetation-agro farming as a model are present in the form of green area.

Now if we face many problem it will be because of lack of the proper planning. All the departments have to sit together and plan for the development of Himalaya. If it is not done, natural calamities will definitely increase. For example, Public Works Department is not consulting Geologists while making roads.

By the development of single species in forest, organic-

diversity is found to be reduced. The insects are affecting the mono forest of sal, shesham, pine, etc. but the crisis is still at low level in the mixed forest farming. Now the scientists are accepting this concept.

Vegetation-agro farming is attracting the birds more. The birds are protecting the trees from insects as they are making them their food. There Nature's call (beat) is more fertile than that of other manure and resulting in more vegetation in the land. These plants include painya, mehal, timla, khaina, chanchari, Kafal, bhimal, kharik and telks. Many people have practically seen the fertility of this land, which was barren earlier.

By growing plants in the land where stones are found in abundance, vegetation-agro farming has succeeded in growing plants (roots) on the height of 1500 meters that grow between 1000 and 3000 mts. As per monsoon adoption, that would help benefiting from agriculturisation of roots and herbs it would solidify the economy of Himalayan states.

A significant success has been achieved in mixed forest farming through 'pit making technique'. In this technique a pit is dug and soil dug out of the pit is spread around it and pit is filled with waste vegetation. A crop is grown/cultivated on this soil with good handsome return. Thus botanical manure is received. Biological agriculture is a need in Uttaranchal. Rainwater goes deep inside the pit resulting water resource in the root of 'mixed forest farming'. During dry season, waste vegetation that converts into good manure, spread out in the field and forest. During rainy season, water crops are also grown in the pits.

Bio-fertilizer may be substitute of chemical fertilizer. It can be flourished with the help of un-employed, women, Government and non-Government organization in the country including Himalayan states.

The percentage of forestland is much more in Himalaya. Conservation of forest and vegetation-agro system is necessary. This farming should be developed with the help of unemployed. It would make them loyal towards the nature and would also stop the fleeing of people from Himalayan's hill station to plains.

With the help of giving-taking and snatch tendency, if we give something to the nature, in one way or the other the nature is responding it to us. But if we try to exploit it in unsystematic manner, the nature suffers great losses and as a result, natural disasters occurs taking a huge toll of human life. Ultimately it affects the development process. Therefore, for the sake of development, the favour of the nature is taken care of simultaneously. The greed of the human is never ever satisfied. Thus the need of Himalayan population should also be taken care of. They must be provided some facilities for protecting security and prosperity of the country as they are depending on the Himalaya.

Many Himalayan states have the tradition of farming by deforestation (shifting cultivation) and developing sloppy treeless farming is being done everywhere. Landslides and floods are but natural in such circumstances. To avoid such a critical situation it will be beneficial to develop mixed forest farming (like vegetation-agro) in the Himalaya as whole.

A large number of botanic diversity in the Himalaya is necessary as 'JAL KUMER' (water resources) are ice or be present in the areas of botanic diversity and there would be no crisis of water, 'JAL-KUBER' are present in the Himalaya. It is good that the people have come forward for this and to act accordingly. They have a concern about environment and this has taken birth in their mind. If it is done, it would help in keeping the environment clean and would support in managing the natural disasters.

Table 12.0 : List of Vegetation Grown and Found in the Vegetation : Agro System at Kot Malla Village, Rudraprayag, Garhwal Himalaya

Type of Vegetation	*Varieties/Species (Names in capital Hindi/Garhwali)*
Fodder	BANJ / OAK (Quereus incana), BHIMAT (Grewk oppostifolia), KHADIK (Celtis australis), KHAIRA (Ficuscunia), TIMLA (Ficus Roxburghii), ROBANIA (Robinia Labeek), THELKA (Fi cusnerifolia), SADAR (Ougeinia oojeinensis), KATCHNAR (Bauhinia variegata), ONGA (Hovenia dulcis), MANIPURI BANJ (Manipuri oak), DHAULA (Woodfordia floribunda), BEDU (Ficus palmata), CHANCHARI (Senecio rufinervis), BHANDIR (Acer oblonguam), HAIRIGH (Quereus glanca), MAALU (Bauhinia vahlii), BILAIMATI BABUL (Acacia farnessiana), CHAMLAI (Desmodium Teliadefolium), PAIEYA (Prunus cerasoides), CHAMKHARIK (Lefger stromeia indie), UTTIS.
Fuel and Furniture	CHIR/ PINE (Pinus roxburghii), VIDESICHIR (Pinus petrola), KAIL (Pinus, wallichiana), DEVDAR (Cedrus deodara), SURA (Cupressus torulosa), SAGAUN (Tectona grandis), SHISHAM (Dalbergia sissoo), TUNGLA (Rhusparviflora), ASIN (Terminalia tomentosa), ANGHU (Fraxinus micranthus), PANGAR (Aesculus indica), ANYAR (Lyonia ovalifolies), TUN (Cedrela toona), RINGAL (Dendrocalamus stricuius), BANS (Bambusa arundinarea), BANS CHINA (Phyllosta chysaurea), BANS PILA (Bambusa vulgaris).

Fruit and Medicinal Plants	JAMUN (Syzygium cumini), CHUYRA (Deploknema butyracia), KAPHAL (Myrica esajlanta), KEEMU (Moursalba), MEHAL (Pyru; pashia), HARSINGAR (Nectanchies arbotristis), REETHA (Sapmdusmukorossi), JATTOON (Ole cuspidate), HRIRA (Teimmalea chebula), AVANLA (Playllanthus embhela), AKHROT (Juglans regra), BADAM (Prunus amygdalus varsatova), KEENU (Citrus retaliate varkimu), NIMBU (Citrus medica), NASHPATI (Pyrus cummunis), ASHOK (Saraca indica), Horse Chestnut (Aesculus hippocaeianum), AARU (Prunus persica), DALCHINI (Cimmamomum tamala), BURASH (Rhodooendron arboreum), RUDRAKSH (Eloeocarpus ganitrus), THUNER (Taxus bacate) (Under successful experiment), TIMRU (Zanthoxylum arimatum), GAITI (Boehmeria rugulosa), THAK (Butea frondosa), UTTIS (Alnusnepalensis), BHOTTA BADAM (Corylus colurna), PIPAL (Ficus religiosa), BAINT (Cane).
Cash Crops	GAUNCHI (Mucuna prurita), BHAISLO (Mucuna nigricans), TIMRY (Zaothoxylun armatum), PAHARIPUDINA (Mentha spicata), BARIELAICHI (Elettris cardamom), CHOTIELAICHI (Zingber officianale).

Herbs	INDRAYAN/ILARU (Curcuma lpnga), CHAI, Tea (Camellia sinenisis), HALDI (Curcuma longa) (Trichosanthes tricuspidata), PASAN BHEID (Bergenia ciliata), SILPHARI (B.stracheyi), PKRPHURIA (Digitalis purpurea), KINGORA (Berberis affstala), SAMEVA/TAGAR (Valeriana hardwickii), BAJARDANTI (Potentilla falgence), GILOYA(Tinospora cordifolia), TULSI (Aximum sactun), SATAVAR/JHIRAN (Asperegus racemosus), KESAR (Crocu; sativis), SHANKPUSPI (Evolvulus alanoides), CHIRAYATA (Suarsia chirayata), KANDALI/BICHHU GHASS (Urtica ardens), ALMORA (Rurnex histatus), CHIPARI (Vitis himalayana), MAKGYA/KAKMACHI (Salanum mgrum), BRAHMI (Centella asiatica), BACH/BACHA (Acorus calamnus), LANGLI (Gloriosa superba), MEISALAKRI (Litses glutmoca), KAULKAND/BANPYAZ (Urginiea Indica), QINDAURI (Stephania glaora), PA.HARI PAN (Piper betle), SALAMPANZA (Dactylorhiza hatagirea), VANKAKRI (Podophyllum bexandrum), KUT (Saussurea lappa), NEIRPATTI (Skimmia anquitifolia), DHRUT KUMARI (Adohaera).

Biofenching Vine etc.	(Dropteris marginata), NERPHARN (Dryopteris odontzlomal NERPHARN (Schimperiana). SINVALI (Vitexnegundo), KUNZA (Rosa Brunonii), KARONZA (Carissia opaca), RAMBANS (Agave cantala), HINSALU (Rubusellipticus), NAGPHANI (Opuntia vulgaris), SEIM (Dolichos lab-lab), DUDLYA (Buddleja asiatica), DUDIBEIL (Vallaris silanacea), GEINTHIBEIL (Dioscorea bulbifera).
Flowers	GEINDA (Tagetus jndicus), GULAB (Rosa iridica), GULAB (Rosa damascena), BULGARIAN ROSE (Rosa bulgarian), RED ROD (Red rod), GOODHULL (Hibisucs rosa-sinensis), DAHLIA (Dahlia), GAZANIA (Gazania), LILI (Lilium giganticum), all local flowers.
Others	Spices (Cardamom, Ginger etc.) Pulses (Rajma, Soyabean etc.) and Vegetables (Tori, Radish, Kulffa. Palake etc.)

Source : Authors and Kodiyal.

Conclusion

Vegetation-agro system or mixed forest farming has a deep understanding with the nature. It may play a great role in natural disaster management like landslide and floods. It is a strong way to meet the challenges between human being and environment. Vegetation-agro system may also play a vital role in the sustainable development of the Himalaya. One new dimension of this system is coming up in the form of recharge of one small spring.

All the geographers, ecologists, scientists, environmentalists, Government and Non-Government Organisations, dynamic farmers, active local social workers, etc. must work for the protection of the Himalaya. It is hope that all the persons will extend their esteemed support for the development of vegetation-agro system in different parts of the country particularly in mountains. In this regard, we would like to say that Dr. Mohan Singh Panwar, President DKD (Friends of tree) and Reader in Department of Geography, H.N. Bahuguna University, Srinagar, Pauri Garhwal (Uttaranchal) has initiated the above quoted model of vegetation-agro system at Maloo Pani village of Tehri Garhwal district.

Acknowledgement

We are thankful to Shri B.S.Rawat, Chief Development Officer, District Rudraprayag (Uttaranchal) for imitating to develop this model at village Kodima, Uttaranchal. It is the privilege of local that Dr. Mohan Singh Panwar, Dr. Mishra, Dr. Kaushal Kumar Sharma (University of Delhi), Dr. N.P.Singh, Dr. Punyatoya Patra, Dr. B.W. Pandey, Dr. V.S.Negi, Dr. Poonam Kumari, Dr. R.B. Singh and students of University of Delhi and Garhwal are encouraging and participating in work from time to time. We are also thankful to Mrs. Sita Devi (Aunti of Mr. Jagat Singh Chaudhary) for guidance, Mrs. Shanti Devi, (wife of Mr. Jagat Singh Chaudhari) Mrs. Krishna Bandooni, Dr. Sarita Panwar and Mrs. Janki Devi. Last, but not the least we are highly grateful to Hon'ble Ex-Governor of Uttaranchal, Shri Surjeet Singh Barnala and Chief Secretary of Uttaranchal, Dr. R.S. Tolia for providing moral, financial and other supports.

References

Bandooni, S.K. 2004 : Land Resource Management and Development in Hill Areas, Research India Press, New Delhi.

Joshi, D.P., 1984 : 'Forests and Frirral/Development in Himalayas Hlliteions of U.P.' in S.C. Joshi et al. (Eds) Rural Development in the Himalaya : Problem and prospects, Gyanodaya Prakashan, Nainital, pp- 79-86.

Kandari, O.P. and Gusain, O.P. 2001 : Garhwal Himalaya : Nature, Culture and Society, Transmedia, Srinagar.

Kodiyal et al. 1990 : Parvatiya Vriksh, Jharinya Va Gasein, HARK, Dehradun, pp. I-XVII.

Shiva, M.P., 1994 : Jari Buntiyan Evam Massala, Centre of Minor Forest Products, Dehradun, pp. 63-98.

Wajton, H.G. 1910 : British Garhwal; A Gazetteer, Govt. Press, Allahabad.

CHAPTER 13

El-Nino Causes and It's Impacts on Environment

DR. S. L. CHOPRA AND MUKESH KUMAR CHOPRA

Lecturer of Geography, Govt.SSS,Kishanpura,Jaipur.

Introduction

Weather and climate have profound influence on life on earth. Climate is determined by the atmospheric circulation and by its interaction with large-scale ocean current and the land. The growth movement and decay of weather systems depend on the vertical structure of the atmosphere, land and sea. There seems to be frequent changes in the climate pattern distribution across the globe. These changes are largely influenced by the human interventions. Based on climatic variations, Scientists have predicted that these calamities are yet to come around the globe.

The onset of El-Nino is marked by abnormal weather patterns that drastically affect the economies of Ecuador and Peru. These unusually warm current amass large quantities of warm water in the eastern Pacific. This warm pool blocks the upwelling of colder, nutrient-filled water and the anchovies starve from lack of food, devastating the local economies. Yet at the same time, some inland areas that are normally arid receive an uncommon abundance of rain. Here, pastures and cotton fields have yields far above the norm. These climatic fluctuations have been known for years, but were always considered local phenomena. Today, we know that El-Nino is a part of the global circulation and affects the weather at great distances from Peru and Ecuador.

El-Nino is one such climate variation due to warm current invasion in the South and Central American coastal waters. This unexpected warm water causes change in fish populations, rainfall and weather across North and South America. The Major highlights of such happenings are brought to light. El-Nino mostly affects the hydrosphere and the atmosphere. El-Nino events occur about every four to seven years and typically last for around 12 to 18 months. They are natural part of the climate system and have been affecting the pacific basin for thousands of years.

Near the end of each year, a weak, warm counter current flows southward along the coasts of Ecuador and Peru, replacing the cold Peruvian current (Humboldt Current). Centuries ago the local residents named this annual event El-Nino ("the child") after the Christ child because it usually appeared during the Christmas season. Normally, these warm countercurrents last for almost a few weeks when they again give way to the cold Peruvian flow. However, every three to seven years, this countercurrents is unusually warm and strong. Accompanying this event is a pool of warm, ocean surface water in the central and eastern Pacific. Today, Scientists use the term **El-Nino** for these episodes of ocean that originally bore the name.

Causes of El-Nino

Energy and matter are exchanged regularly between the sea and the land. Much of this interchange occurs by atmospheric processes, as wind/air masses sweep across land water, transporting gases, solid and liquid particles, and heat across the globe, an example of one such global linkage is the peculiar nature of weather worldwide that accompanies the occurrence of a strong El-Nino offshore Peru. At first oceanographers tended to treat El-Nino as a regional event, not realizing that its cause is located far away in the equatorial Pacific and that its ramifications are truly global in extent. Let's explore our current understanding of this climate/marine phenomenon. During a strong El-Nino event, warm, nutrient-poor tropical water displaces the normal cold, nutrient-rich water of the Peruvian continental shelf. This leads to economic catastrophe as the anchovy fisheries in the area collapses. One of the strongest El-Nino events on record occurred in 1982-83 and was accompanied by major weather disturbances worldwide. To name a few, they included record rainfall in Ecuador and north-western Peru (a desert); drought in the agricultural sectors of Bolivia and southern Peru; Severe drought in eastern Australia, Indonesia, and southern India, southern Africa; an unusual number of typhoons (hurricanes) in the southern Pacific Ocean; and severe coastal storms along California, drought in the north central states, and mild winters in the eastern parts of the United States.

Scientists discovered that changes in the flow pattern of the south-east trade winds trigger El-Nino. Normally, the south-east trade winds flow vigorously from a high-pressure zone in the eastern pacific to a low-pressure zone in the western pacific. These strong and persistent winds drag warm water westward and pile it against South-east Asia. Under these conditions, the sea surface slopes up to the west and cold, nutrient-rich water occurs in the eastern equatorial Pacific and upwells along Peru. At times, such as 1982-83 the atmospheric pressure gradient that controls the trade winds breaks down, and air pressure rises in the eastern Pacific and drops in the western Pacific. This causes the trades to slacken and sometimes to even reverse direction, so that equatorial winds now blow from west. Then, warm surface water is dragged eastward by these anomalous winds. This raises sea level in the eastern Pacific and lowers it in the western Pacific, and allows warm, nutrient-poor water to flow against South America replace.

- Amazon rainforests turning into desert.
- Occurrence of forest fires in the Northern regions and Tropics.
- Melting of ice caps of Arctikc and Siberian.
- Changing Monsoon phenomena.

Impacts of El-Nino Occurrences on Marine Life

The key element of the El-Nino phenomenon is the interaction between the sea surface and wind. The effects from El-Nino Southern Oscillation have an impact on fisheries and marine life, as well as climatic conditions around the globe. As the surface water moves away from the west to east in slow wave, the boundary between warm surface water and deep cold water known as thermocline depresses in the east and elevates in the west. This phenomenon is called upwelling. The coastal upwelling is no longer able to tap into the cold nutrient-rich water from beneath it, thus reducing the supply of chemical nutrients to the euphotic zone. As a result of this decrease in nutrients there is drastic decline in phytoplankton production which in turn adversely affects all the creatures at higher level of the marine food chain.

On Fisheries

The greatest biological impact of El-Nino is upon the fisheries in the coastal region of the eastern pacific. The decline in coastal upwelling causes a reduction in primary productivity which in turn decreases the food available to the natural fish population. During El-Nino, when the above event combines, with an increase in sea surface temperature, it encourages fish located in the costal areas to migrate north and south in search of cooler waters and food. Fish unable to migrate die from lack of food or due to intolerable temperature elevation. Another factor of El-Nino that alters coastal fish population is the increase in the rainfall along the Southern American coast. This results in an increase turbidity and increased salinity from enhanced river discharge which brings with it large amounts of sediments and fresh water. The fish either leave their coastal habitat or die from endurable water conditions.

On Fauna

In the Weddell seal population in Antarctica researchers noticed that the number of births decline every four to six years coinciding with the El-Nino events. The decline in the seal population may be due to the changes in the fish population caused by the shifts in the ocean currents. In 1982-83 El-Nino events, a dramatic reduction in the number of California Sea Lions occurred at Santa Catalina island California. During the same, it has been estimated that upto 85% of the sea bird population of Peru were killed. Some of the factors that contribute to the decline in their populations are :

- Flooding of nesting sites.
- Changing atmospheric circulation patterns.
- Increasing sea surface temperature. and
- Migration of their primary food source, fish.

Oceanic Drift Leading to New Ecosystem

Some marine creatures also benefits from the disturbances brought upon the phenomenon of El-Nino. As a result of 1982-83 El-Nino, Scallops accelerated their growth and reached high densities. Purple Snails, Octopuses and the shrimp became more common. Fishery reached its highest level. This may be due to the result of increased runoff from rivers, increased rainfall which provided a greater abundance of nutrients and decreased predation from a dispersed fish population.

Ecological imbalance

In 1982-83, El-Nino was responsible for the ecological effects on other marine resources. The eastern Pacific region suffered massive coral bleaching events and mortalities that have tragic results for the coral reef community. The increased sea surface temperature and the rainfall induced salinity changes in the water are considered to be the underlying causes for the declination of the coral reef community in this region. In the western Pacific, the decrease in sea level was responsible for exposing and destroying the upper layers of the coral reefs that surround many islands.

Economic Impacts of El-Nino

Dry condition in 1982-83 El-Nino events, Indonesia suffered $ 500 million in drought and fire. Dry condition also in Australia resulted in a $ 2 million loss in crops and millions of cattle dies due to lack of water. In 1991-92, Australian droughts destroyed wheat fields and killed several thousands of millions of tonnes of grains to feed their people due to severe droughts. In 1997, the effects of El-Nino have been seen with massive fires in Indonesia and Australia, drought and famine in Papua New Guinea. Heavy rains and flooding occurred in southern Brazil, Northern Peru, Southern Ecuador and Southern California. The El-Nino 1998 has made one of the driest years on the east coast of North America.

El-Nino-Southern Oscillation (ENSO)

Historically, Peru's residents knew that a current of warm water after every few years reduced the population of anchovies in coastal waters. The decrease in anchovies not only caused a dramatic decline in the fishing industry, it also caused the decline of marine life such as marine mammals and sea birds that depend on anchovies as a source of food. This warm current also brought about changes in the weather-usually intense rainfall and even brought such interesting items as floating coconuts from tropical islands near the Equator. At first, these events were called *anos de abundancia* (years of abundance) because of the increase in plant growth on land due to the increase in rainfall in normally arid regions. What was once thought of as a joyous event, however, soon became associated with the ecological and economic disaster that is now a well-known consequence of the phenomenon.

Figure shows that high pressure (caused by sinking air within the South Pacific High) dominates the coastal region of South America resulting in clear, fair and dry weather conditions. Across the Pacific, rising air within the Indonesians low pressure is responsible for creating cloudy conditions with plentiful precipitation in Indonesia, New Guinea and northern

Australia. This pressure difference causes the strong south-east trade winds to move from high to low pressure across the equatorial South Pacific (see Figure 6-12). The circulation cell in the equatorial South Pacific Ocean created by the movement of air between high and low pressure regions is named the **Walker Circulation Cell** after G.T. Walker a British meteorologist who first described the effect in the 1920.

The warm-water phenomenon usually occurred around Christmas near Peru and Ecuador coast was given the name **El-Nino,** Spanish for "the child" in reference to baby Jesus. Because an El-Nino event is associated with the switching of atmospheric regions called the Southern Oscillation. El-Nino more correctly called **El-Nino–Southern Oscillation (ENSO)** events which indicates the inter-relationship between ocean and atmosphere during such an event.

Figure is a diagrammatic view across the equatorial South Pacific Ocean that shows how normal conditions change as a result of an ENSO. The high pressure along the coast of South America weakens causing a smaller difference in atmospheric pressure between the high and low pressure region of the Walker Circulation Cell. A smaller pressure difference causes the south-east trade winds to diminish or in very strong ENSO events, actually to *blow in the reverse direction.* When the trade winds fail, this is a sure sign of an impending ENSO.

Without the trade winds, the Pacific warm pool that has built up on the western side of the Pacific begins to flow back across the ocean toward South America. This is accomplished by an increase in the flow of the Equatorial Countercurrent. Thus the temperature of surface waters across the Pacific increase as the water flows to the east across the ocean basin toward Peru. This creates a band of warm water that stretches across the equatorial Pacific Ocean. The warm water usually begins to move in September of an ENSO year, and comes into contact with South America by December or January. In strong to very strong ENSO events, the water temperature of Peru can increase by 8 degrees centigrade (14 degrees Fahrenheit) as compared to normal conditions. In addition the presence of warm water along the coast of South America can cause an increase in average sea level by as much as 20 centimeters (8 inches), simply due to thermal expansion of the warm water.

As the warm water moves across the Pacific, sea surface temperatures increase in the equatorial region. This causes a devastating effect on corals because the water temperatures are simply too high for corals to survive. Thus corals are decimated in Tahiti, the Galapagos, and other tropical Pacific islands after the warm water contacts in South America. The warm water also moves north and south, travelling along, the west coast of the Americas and bringing increased average sea level along with it. In addition, the warm water causes an increase in the number of tropical hurricanes formed in the eastern Pacific.

The flow of warm water across the Pacific also causes the sloped thermocline boundary between warm surface waters and the cooler waters below to flatten out and became more horizontal. Near Peru, upwelling brings warmer, nutrient-depleted water to the surface. In fact, *downwelling* can sometimes occur as the warm water stacks up along coastal South America. Thus productivity diminishes and most types of marine life in the area are dramatically reduced.

As the warm water moves to the east across the Pacific, the low pressure zone also migrates. In strong to very strong ENSO events, the low pressure can move entirely across the Pacific and remain over South America. The low pressure causes much precipitation along coastal South America, an area that normally is influenced by high pressure and receives very little precipitation. Conversely, the Indonesian low-pressure region is replaced by a high-pressure region, bringing dry conditions or, in strong to very strong ENSO events, drought conditions to Indonesia and northern Australia. ENSO events usually end 12 to 18 months after they start, with a gradual return to near normal conditions that begins in the south-eastern tropical Pacific and spreads westward.

Effects of ENSOs

Mild ENSO events influence only the equatorial South Pacific Ocean. Strong to very strong ENSO events not only influences the weather in the equatorial South Pacific, but also often can be felt worldwide. Typically, an ENSO will alter the atmospheric jet steam and produce weather *different from normal conditions* in most parts of the globe. Sometimes this manifested as drier than normal conditions; at other times, conditions may be better than normal. In addition, the weather in a region may be warmer or cooler than normal. It still remains a difficult task to predict exactly how a particular ENSO will affect any region's weather.

Figure shows some of the typical effects felt worldwide as a result of very strong ENSO events. Flooding erosion, droughts, fires, tropical storms, and effects on marine life are all associated with ENSO events. These weather perturbations also affect the production of certain commodities such as corn, cotton and coffee. ENSO events are clearly related to other periodic climatic fluctuation observed worldwide, and the relations among these occurrences are being intensely studied to gain further insight into understanding the world's climate.

More locally, the warm water from an ENSO event can work its way along the west coast of the United States all the way to British Columbia. Canada, Figure 7-21 shows satellite images of sea surface temperatures of southern California during a normal and an ENSO year.

Examples from Recent ENSOs

During this century, there have been a number of ENSO events of varying severity (Table 7-13). The average frequency of moderate, strong and very strong ENSO events is one every 2 to 10 years, but in highly irregular pattern. For instance, in some decades there has been an ENSO event after every few years, while in other decades there may have been only one ENSO event. Let's examine some of the effects of some of the more recent ENSOs.

In the winter of 1976, a moderate ENSO event coincided with California's worst drought of this century. Thus, it is clear that ENSO events don't just bring torrential rains to the western United States, during this same winter the eastern United States also experienced cold conditions.

The 1982-1983 ENSO stands as the strongest ENSO events ever recorded causing far-ranging effects across the globe (Figure 7-20). In the United States, the jet stream swung much farther south than normal and brought a series of powerful storms. This caused upto three times the normal rainfall in the south-western United States, which resulted in severe flooding and landslides. Higher than normal sea level combined with high surf caused much damage to coastal structures and an increase in coastal erosion. There was much snowfall across the Rocky Mountains. Alaska and western Canada experienced a warm winter, and the eastern United States had its mildest winter in 25 years, meanwhile, in Europe, there was severe cold weather worldwide, there were droughts in Australia, Indonesia, China, India, Africa and Central America.

In the Pacific Ocean, normally arid Peru was drenched with more than 3 meters (10 feet) of rainfall, causing extreme damage by flooding and landslides. Sea surface temperatures were so high that corals were decimated across the equatorial Pacific. In this region, marine mammals and sea birds that depend on the food source associated with normal high productivity died or went elsewhere. French Polynesia had not experienced a hurricane in 75 years ; that year it also which endured six Kauai also experienced a rare hurricane.

Worldwide there was an estimated $ 8 billion in damage ($2 billion in the United States) and over 1000 deaths were attributed. The 1982-1983 ENSO events can be indicial for some regions. For instance, tropical hurricane formation is generally suppressed in the Atlantic Ocean, some desert regions receive much-needed rain, and organisms adapted to warm-water conditions thrive in the Pacific.

The 1982-83 ENSO event was neither predicted, nor was it recognized until it was near its peak. Because of the extensive damage and worldwide influence on weather phenomena caused by the 1982-83 ENSO event, a major study of the mechanism of ENSO events was to be initiated in 1985, called the **Tropical Ocean-Global Atmosphere (TOGA)** program. The goal of the TOGA program was to monitor the equatorial South Pacific Ocean during the time when ENSO events occurred to enable scientists to model and predict future ENSO events. The 10- year program involved studying the ocean from research vessels, analyzing surface and subsurface data from radio-transmitting sensor buoys, monitoring oceanic phenomena by satellite, and developing computer models. The study was completed in 1995, offering a wealth of new data that has enabled scientist to develop more reliable models that link the combined ocean-atmospheric system. These models have given scientists the ability to predict ENSO events upto a year in advance, as was done for the ENSO events of 1987, 1992 and 1998. Since the completion of TOGA, the **Tropical Atmosphere and Ocean (TAO)** project has continued to monitor the equatorial Pacific Ocean with a series of 70 moored buoys. This multinational project is sponsored by the United States, Canada, Australia, and Japan.

In the fall of 1987, a strong ENSO event started to form but for some reason lost energy. Eventually, it expressed itself as moderate ENSO event.

In 1991-1992 an ENSO event began that produced global weather modifications similar to those of the 1982-83 event. For instance, warm water was found in offshore of California. Heavy rains in the mid-continent region of the United States caused flooding in the Missouri and Mississippi Rivers, and the Pacific North-West and Canada were very dry. TOGA computer models were able to predict this ENSO event even though the causes of ENSO events are still not fully understood. The 1991-1992 ENSO was unusual because it maintained itself until the spring of 1995.

The 1997-1998 ENSO event was unusual in that it began several months earlier than normal and peaked in January 1998. In terms of the amount of Southern Oscillation and sea surface warming in the equatorial Pacific, the 1997-1998 ENSO was initially as strong as the 1982-1983 ENSO, which was the strongest event of the century. However, the 1997-1998 ENSO weakened in the last few months of 1997 before reintensifying in early 1998. The impact of the 1997-1998 ENSO event was felt mostly in the tropical Pacific, where surface water temperatures were upto 8 degrees centigrade (14 degrees Fahrenheit) warmer than normal in eastern Pacific areas such as the Galapagos Islands and off the coast of Peru. In the western Pacific, drought conditions persisted because of the high-atmospheric-pressure system that replaced the area's normal low pressure causing wildfires to burn out of control in Indonesia. Also, there was warmer water than normal along the west coast of Central and North America, which caused an increase in hurricane occurrence of Mexico. In the United States, many unusual weather events were linked to the 1997-1998 ENSO, such as killer tornadoes in the south-east, massive blizzards in the upper Midwest, and flooding of the Ohio River Valley. In California, most of the state received two times the normal rainfall, which caused flooding and landslides in many parts of the state. However, the lower Midwest, the Pacific North-west, and the eastern seaboard had relatively mild weather. In spite of predictions that the 1997-1998 ENSO would be the most severe ENSO of the century it did not affect worldwide weather or cause damage and casualties to the extent that the 1982 -1983 ENSO did.

Indian Ocean Circulation

Because the Indian Ocean is mostly in the Southern Hemisphere (extending only to about 20 degrees north latitude), surface circulation varies considerably from that in the Atlantic and Pacific from November to March, the equatorial circulation is similar to that in the other oceans, with two westward-flowing equatorial currents (North and South Equatorial Currents) separated by an eastward-flowing Equatorial Countercurrent. However, in contrast to the Atlantic and Pacific wind systems, which shift northward of the geographical Equator, the meteorological equator is shifted southward in the Indian Ocean.

The Equatorial Countercurrent flows between 2 and 8 degrees south latitude, bounded on the north by the North Equatorial Current (which extends as far as 10 degrees north latitude) and on the south by the South Equatorial Current (which extends to 20 degrees south latitude). The winds of the northern Indian Ocean have a seasonal pattern that are called **monsoon** (monsoon= season) winds.

During winter, the typical north-east trade winds are called the north-east monsoon. They are strengthened by the rapid cooling of air over the Asian mainland during winter. This creates a high-pressure which is less (green arrows in figure7-22 A).

During summer, the Asian mainland warms faster than the adjacent ocean. As a result a summer low pressure air develops over the continent allowing higher-pressure air to reverse direction and move from the Indian Ocean.

Recall that this is due to the lower heat capacity of continental rocks and soil compared with water onto the Asian landmass. This gives rise to the south-west monsoon (green arrows in figure 7-22B), which may be thought of as a continuation of the south-east trade winds across the Equator. During this season, the North Equatorial Current disappears and is replaced by the south-west Monsoon Current. It flows from west to east across the North Indian Ocean. In September or October, the north-east trade winds are re-established, and the North Equatorial Current reappears (Figure 7-22A).

Surface circulation in the southern Indian Ocean (the **Indian Ocean Gyre)** is similar to the counter clock-wise circulation of gyres observed in other southern ocean when the north-east trade winds blow. The South Equatorial Current provides water for the Equatorial Countercurrent and the **Agulhas Current,** which flows southward along Africa's eastern coast and joins the West Wind Drift. Turning northward out of the West Wind Drift is the **West Australian Current,** an eastern boundary current that completes the gyre by merging with the South Equatorial Current.

During the South-west monsoon, a northward flows from the Equator along the coast of Africa, the **Somali Current,** develops with velocities approaching 4 kilometers (2.5 miles) per hour.

The eastern boundary current in the southern Indian Ocean is unique. Other eastern boundary currents of subtropical gyres are cold drifts towards the Equator that produce arid coastal climates, which receive less than 25 centimeters (10 inches) of rain per year. However, in the Southern Indian Ocean, the West Australian Current is displaced offshore by a southward-flowing current called the **Lenin Current** is driven southward along the Australian coast from the warm water dome piled up in the East Indies by the Pacific Equatorial Current.

The Leeuwin Current produces a mild climate in south-western Australian which receives about 125 centimeters (50 inches) of rain per year. This Current weakens during ENSO events and contributes to Australian drought conditions associated with these events.

Future Implication of El-Nino

Globally there seems to be changes in the wind and sea patterns. These effects require utmost attention since the seasonal and ecological imbalances resulted in serious economic losses. El-Nino can be predicted using scientific models to know how the ocean atmosphere system might evolve over the next seasons or years. By inter-relating the prediction models with the management decisions, humankind would be able to adopt better to the irregular rhythms of climate. To respond to the impact of an unexpected El-Nino by using measures such as closing the fishing season after the population has declined, will continue to be ineffectual and costly, thereof understanding these seasonal imbalances in the ocean will definitely help us to overcome serious losses and also to explore its usage in farming, tourism, health and many other fields.

References

Allan, Rob *et al.* : El-Nino Southern Oscillation and Climate variety (CSIRO, 1996).

Diaz, H.F. and Markgraf, Vera eds. El-Nino: Historical and Paleo-climatic Aspects of the Southern Oscillation, Cambridge Univ. Press. 1992.

Gland, M.H. 1996 : Currents of change: El-Nino's Impact on Climate and Society.

Horst, E.J. 1997 : Impact of El-Nino on winter weather in Lancaster, Summary Outlook for winter trenberth.

K.E. and Hear T.J. 1996 : El-Nino Southern Oscillation event Longeston record: Geographical Research Letters, V. 23 pp. 57-60.

Thompson, D.W.J., and Solomon, S. 2002 : Interaction of recent Southern Hemisphere Climate change, Sinces, 296 895-899.

Pinet, R. Panl, 1998 : Invitation to oceanography Johes as Borkt London.

Lutgen, F.K. and Tubnk, E.J. 1998 : The Atmosphere prentice hall New Jersey.

Thurman, H.V. and Trujillo, A.P. 1999 : Essentials of Oceanography, Prentice Hall, New Jersey.

Gurjar, R.K. and Jat, B.C. 2005 : Environmental Geography, Panchsheel Prakashan , Jaipur .

Jat, B.C. and Mathur Sujata, 2006 : Environmental studies Panchsheel Prakashan, Jaipur.

Murray Mitchell, J : El-Nino the Global Weather Connection" Weather-wise 36, no. 4 (August 1983) 168.

Glantz, M.H. 1996 : Currents of change El-Nino's impact on climate and society Cambridge University Press.

National Research Council. 1996 : Leaning to predict climate variations associated with El-Nino and the southern oscillation: Accomplish-ments and legacies of the TOGA program. Washington. DC. National Academy Press.

Pedlosky, J. 1990 : The dynamics of the oceanic subtropical gyres. Science 248:4935316-322.

Philander, S.G. 1996 : El-Nino and La Nina. In Price, R.G. ed., Oceanography: Contemporary readings in ocean sciences 3rd ed., New York: Oxford University Press.

Philander, S.G. 1992 : El-Nino Oceans 35:2, 56-61.

Philander, S.G. 1983 : El-Nino Southern Oscillation phenomena Nature 302:5906, 295-301.

The Open University Course Team, 1989 : Ocean Circulation Oxford Pergamon Press.

University Corporation for Atmospheric Research 1994 : El-Nino and climate prediction Reports to the Nation on our changing Planet Spring 1994 No. 3.

Davidson, K. 1995 : El-Nino Strikes again 4:3, 24-33. A look at production of and destruction caused by the lingering 1994 ENSO event.

Knox, P.N. 1992 : El-Nino - A current catastrophe 1:5, 30-37, Discusses various weather phenomena that are related to ENSO events, and focuses on unusual weather in 1992 that was the result of an ENSO.

Sobey, E. 1982 : What is sea level ? 28:3, 136-142 : The factors that cause sea level to change are discussed.

Whitchead, J.A. 1989 : Giant Ocean cataract 2602:50 57. An examination of the effect on ocean circulation of giant ocean cataracts which are large and fast flows of deep water that play a crucial role in maintaining the chemistry and climate of the deep ocean.

CHAPTER 14

Fluoride Toxicity an Alarming Hazards in Developing World

MAHESHWARI R[1], RAANI B[2]
[1]Department of Chemistry, SBDTC, Lakshman Garh (Sikar), Rajasthan
[2]Department of Chemistry, PIET,RIICO(IA),ISI 2, Jaipur, Rajasthan

1. Introduction

Fluoride is known to contaminate groundwater reserves globally. Fluorosis, though a common endemic problem of our country is more widespread and acute in Rajasthan, where all the 32 districts are engulfed by the clutches of fluorosis, to a varying degree. Besides India, the countries that are affected more include Pakistan, Bangladesh, Argentina, Mexico, Japan, New Zealand, Thailand, USA and East & South Africa. In India its occurrence in top aquifer system is endemic in 19 states viz. Andhra Pradesh (16), Assam (2), Bihar (5), Chattisgarh (2), Delhi (7), Gujarat (18), Haryana (12), Jammu & Kashmir (1), Jharkhand (4), Karnataka (16), Kerala (3), Madhya Pradesh (14), Maharashtra (10), Orissa (18), Punjab (17), Rajasthan (32), Tamil Nadu (8), Uttar Pradesh (7) and West Bengal (4) of India. The number in parenthesis is the total number of district confirmed for fluoride endemicity (Susheela, 2006). Rajasthan (the largest state in the country in terms of geographic spread) has an area of 3.42 lakh Sq kms (10.41% of the country's area) and 5.5% of nation's population but has low water resources (1% of the country's resources). With rising population and depleted groundwater resources, the groundwater quality is deteriorating day by day. As the water table is receding more and more, water sources are becoming prone to higher F-concentration. As per WHO report,

20 per cent of the F-affected villages in the world are in India. Out of 33,211 fluoride-affected villages in the country, Rajasthan has 16,560 villages, which is >51%. From these figures we can draw an inference that nearly 10% of fluoride-affected habitation in the world are in Rajasthan alone. Obviously, groundwater is the major source of potable water and over 94% of the potable water demand is met by groundwater. In 21st century depleting groundwater levels and deteriorated quality will be a major health and environmental problem. The social, economic and environmental values associated with groundwater are often unrecognized. Thus it appears that situation vis-à-vis fluoride is on the rise despite substantial efforts by the government and NGOs activity in the field. The situation is grim and warrants a holistic approach to ameliorate the situation and a concerted action accordingly.

2. Sources of Fluoride Ion in Environment

Fluorine (13th most abundant element of halogen family with At No-9 and MoWt-19) accounts for 0.3 g/kg of earth's crust. Fluorine is the most electronegative of all the elements and exists as a diatomic molecule with a remarkably low dissociation-energy (38k cal/mole). As a result it is highly reactive and has strong affinity to combine with other elements to produce compounds known as fluorides. It is, in fact, one of the most bones seeking acute toxin of notable chemical qualities and physiological properties as well. The main occurrence of fluorine in rocks is in the form of F-bearing minerals. Fluorspar (Sedimentary rocks like limestones, sandstones), Topaz, Villuamite, Cryolite (Igneous rocks like Granite) and Fluoroapatite are the main minerals, which are rich in fluoride. When water percolates it leaches out the F from these minerals (Maheshwari *et al.*, 2006[a]).

Fluorides come next to sulphur dioxide in the hierarchy of atmospheric gaseous pollutants. Fluorides are released in the air as gaseous hydrogen fluoride and volatile fluorides like cryolites and silicon fluoride. These pollutants result from Al factories, brick kiln, pottery industries and ferro-enamel works. Inorganic fluorine compounds are used for producing aluminium. Fluorine is also released during manufacture and use of phosphatic fertilizers in groundwater of zones rich in F-containing minerals, level upto 85 mg/l has been noticed (Maheshwari *et al.*, 2006[b]).

Fluoride ions remain distributed in the atmosphere originating from the dust of F-bearing soils, the domestic burning of coal fires and from gases released in areas of volcanic activities. The F-content in air reach a level as high as 1.4 mg/m^3 and in the neighborhood of such factories a level of 0.2 mg/m^3 gets attained. Problems have occurred while mining of phosphate and fluorspar when dust has been blown over a long distance by the wind and deposited on plants thereby entering the food chain. The use of pesticides containing F has a similar effect, and their use must be monitored and limited strictly. As regards soil and surface water, the use of fertilizers and the discharge of industrial waste into streams are main sources of F-contamination (Maheshwari, *et al.*, 2006[c]).

Studies have shown that significant amount of F is absorbed by brushing teeth with toothpaste (the originally fluoridated toothpastes containing SnF_2 and $Sn_2P_2O_7$), and some detrifrices containing F typically at the level of 1 g/kg. Mouth rinses and tablets containing NaF to be used as anti-carcinogenic agent were found to provide substantial amount of F to the body (Rock and Sabiena, 1997). Medicament, cosmetics and fluoride rich food items are also a source of F for human consumption; some of these are tea, pan, supari, green garlic, onion, cabbage, soybeans, carrot, corn and potato. Prolonged use of certain drugs has been associated with the chronic adverse effects of fluoride e.g. sodium fluoride for treatment of Osteoporosis, Ni-fluoric acid for the treatment of rheumatoid arthritis and the use of mouth rinses. The use of fluorides in industries can often lead to occupational exposure e.g. inorganic F-compounds are used in the production of aluminium and phosphatic fertilizers. Aquatic fauna e.g. fish and some food stuffs e.g. tea, tobacco, spinach, ladyfinger, cauliflower contribute to a high amount of fluoride.

The toxicity of F is influenced by high ambient temperatures, alkalinity, Ca and Mg content in water (Raani, 2004). Climatic conditions play a major role in deciding the extent of F in groundwater. For instance a 2002 research article "Fluoride in shallow aquifers in Raj Garh Tehsil of Churu district, Rajasthan-an arid environment" – published in esteemed journal Current Science points out that "the arid climate with high evaporations and insignificant natural recharge might have accelerated the strengthening of F-concentration in the groundwater of Churu district. In the vast geographical expanse and varied geographical set-up in Rajasthan the cause of fluoridation of groundwater are many some natural, some human-made".

3. Extent of Fluorosis in Rajasthan (Worst Affected Districts viz. Jaipur, Jalore, Nagaur & Churu)

Fluoride ions affect the human physiological system severely. Its low concentration has been used as therapeutic agent in dental caries but excess intake (>1.5 ppm; WHO-1996) causes were health hazards. In our study area, large number of individuals were observed with dental, skeletal and secondary neurological complications. Keeping in view the toxicity caused by F, water samples of different sources were randomly collected from various locations falling in our study zones and analyzed for F-content.

Groundwater samples from 16 villages of Phagi tehsil (Jaipur), 5 villages (Jalore), 5 villages of Didwana block (Nagaur) and 8 villages of Mulsisar block (Churu), collected directly in sterilized polythene bottles (500 ml) were analyzed by Spand's method [Sodium-2- (para-sulphophenylazo)-1,8-dihydroxy-3, 6-naphthelene disulphonate] and Selective Ion Meter (Mettler Toledo M 235 pH/ion analyzer). Standard procedure (APHA, AWWA and WPCF, 1995) was followed for the determination of F-concentration.

Nagaur district of Rajasthan has been known for excessive concentration of F in groundwater. Due to the lack of surface water resources, and semi-arid climatic conditions, increase in groundwater fed irrigated agriculture and erection of a number of groundwater abstraction structures for public water supply, the meager groundwater resources of the district are in the heavy stress. In the villages of Nagaur district, the effects of high F-concentration are severe. Presence of excess F in groundwater has drawn attention of the society due to its pathophysiological impact on human body. F-content in the villages of Nagaur district has been found in the range of 1-62 ppm. Over-exploitation of water resources in the Didwana block has resulted in the depletion of groundwater table, salination of aquifers and deterioration in chemical quality of groundwater at an alarming rate. Therefore, study area is recommended to adopt adequate measures for conservation and judicious management of groundwater resources.

In Jarna Khurd village 20 km away from the city of Jaipur, there are no youth. All 1200 people irrespective of age look old and have cracked teeth. Their shoulders, hips and ankles are swollen and ache all the time. It is painful to stand up, if they squat on the floor. In Jalore, the F-content in water has increased to 6.8 mg/l as against the permissible limit of 1.5 mg/l causing premature aging in the people. Nearly 120 out of 728 villages in the district are in the grip of fluorosis with some of the villages being the worst hit. Osteoporosis, bone deformation and yellowing of teeth are rampant. Even the unborn children are not safe. People are alarmingly dependent on aquifers for their drinking needs.

The area 20 km away from famous marble city Makrana, having 60 villages has been known as Banka-Patti because most of the people of this fluorotic belt are facing skeletal deformities due to consumption of F-rich water. Most of the people of Tedhasar village of Churu district seem to be totally handicapped due to F poisoning. In Mulsisar block of Jhunjhunu district, large number of patients suffering from skeletal fluorosis have been seen. It was also observed that 1 mg of F in potable water dissolve 180 mg of Al, when boiled in an utensil made of aluminium. Generally in rural areas and amongst poorer people, use of Al utensils is quite common feature. Staining, mottling and abrasion of teeth, high F levels in bone and urine, decreased milk production, lameness and sluggishness are some toxic effects observed in cattles grazing around F sources as ceramic rocks, phosphatic fertilizer plants and Al factories (Maheshwari and Bansal, 2006).

4. Fluoride Standards

In 1984, the WHO gave a guideline value of 1.5 ppm as the maximum permissible level for F in potable water. This reflected the state of research on fluoride. A certain amount was considered good for human health but more research changed this attitude. According to UNICEF studies "fluoride has no beneficial health effects. Rather, F destroys teeth. Fluoride has no role in prevention of dental caries, which is basically a bacterial disorder." WHO guideline value is unsafe for some countries. In tropical countries such as India, people drinks more water hence consume more fluoride. Also many food items have high concentration of fluoride. In accordance with a report of a national sanitary engineer, WHO-New Delhi "WHO only gives guidelines. The Indian Government is free to notify its own acceptable limits, the reason being that Indian population is already exposed to F through many sources." During an International workshop on F and defluoridation held in Cheang-Mai (Thailand) 20-24 November 2000, it was recommended that WHO should reduce its guideline value from 1.5 mg/l to 0.5 mg/l. The permissible limit as laid down by the USPH potable water standards and ISI are 1.5 mg/l and 3.0 mg/l respectively. The ISI value available for F level in domestic water supplies is just double as prescribed by UPSH, obviously for no good reasons. "Setting up guidelines for F in water requires carrying out large-scale epidemiological studies. No, such studies have been carried out in India", in accordance with a report of RGNDWM, 1993. BIS prescribed the acceptable limit of 1 mg/l F in potable water in 1992. But this does not mean that it is safe. Malnourished children can be affected even at F levels are below

1 mg/l says UNICEF. Moreover F standards are canonically vague. There exists an "acceptable level" 1 mg/l. But there also exist a cause of rejection level (1.5 mg/l) the water may not be acceptable in the absence of an alternative and better source. Thus, it is shocking and yet legal that the Government continues to follow the 1.5 mg/l limits in its water programmes.

5. Pathophysiological and Biochemical Impact

Human can tolerate F-ions upto 1.0 - 1.5 mg/l depending upon the nutritional status and the physiological aspects of the body. It is roughly estimated that 60% of the total intake is through potable water. Fluoride ions from soluble F-compounds present in water are ingested and are rapidly absorbed through entire GI tract and lungs. The rapid excretion takes place through renal system over a period of 4 to 6 hour in children (3 years of age only) about 50% of total absorbed amount is excreted, but in adults and children over 3 years – about 90% is excreted. Upto the age of 50 yrs, F-content increases in the body, being circulated through the body fluids. Considerable amount of fluoride get deposited in calcified tissues and consequently some portion of F gets excreted through sweat and urine. Number of factors viz. level of different hormones, functioning efficiency of kidney, climatic conditions, previous history of the F exposure of a person and nutritional status influence the excretion process. The rate of retention decreases with age and most of the adults are regarded for practical purpose as imbalance (Maheshwari, 2004).

Fluorine is highly corrosive and its oxidation potential (+2.87V) is even > ozone. It oxidizes water to oxygen and itself gets reduced to F-ions, incorporating into the enamel during mineralization stage of tooth formation and also by surface adsorption after the tooth has erupted. It strengthens dental structure by substituting hydroxyl ions ($-OH^-$) in hydroxyapatite. Resulted Ca- fluorohydroxy apatite, which bears less porous, resists to physico-chemical damages taking place.

$$F_2 + 3H_2O \longrightarrow 2H_3O^+ + 2F^- + H_2O$$

$$[3Ca_3(PO_4)_2.Ca(OH)_2] + 2F^- \longrightarrow 3Ca_3(PO_4)_2.CaF_2$$

Soluble fluorides are readily absorbed in the GIT after ingested through water. Presence of F in water (< 1.5 ppm) results in substantial reduction of dental caries in both children and adults. Once the F is incorporated into the tooth, reduces solubility of the enamel under acidic conditions and provides protection against bacterial disorder creating dental caries, has been found to decrease dental caries upto the level of 1ppm. Mottling of teeth has been observed even to an objectionable degree when the level increased from 1.5 to 2.0 ppm. Skeletal deformities have been noticed when in the people consuming water containing F > 3 to 6 ppm. Cases of crippling skeletal deformities have been observed in the people consuming water > 10 ppm over a long period (Mittal *et al.*, 1993).

The amount of F entering in the hard tissues (e.g. bones) depends upon the several factors viz. F-intake, sex, age, bone type and the specific part of the bone. Due to skeletal growth young one perhaps store more of the daily intake than older one. This observation partially explains the faster removal of F-ions from the plasma of individual. Bones and teeth having highest amount of Ca [in the form of $Ca_3(PO_4)_2$] attract F-ions and form calcium fluoride (Maheshwari, 2006).

$$Ca^{++} + 2F^- \longrightarrow CaF_2$$

Maximum deleterious effects are detected in the neck, knee, pelvic (hip), and pectoral (shoulder) joints. People with the hunchback have also been observed in Mulsisar block of Jhunjhunu district. Fluoride in extra cellular fluids enters the apatite in 3 stages (ion exchange process).

- Fluoride enters the hydration shell (which surrounds the small crystals of bone mineral-hydroxyapatite) and remains in equilibrium with those of the surrounding tissue fluids and apatite crystals.

- Exchange between the fluids of hydration shell and the –OH groups at the crystal surface occurs.
- As a result of recrystalization, some of the F migrate deeper into the matrix thereby gets incorporated into the hard tissues.

6. Chemobiokinetics of Fluorosis

Calcium in the bone exist in form of hydroxyapatite $[Ca_5(OH)(PO_4)_3]$ which forms needle shaped crystals and composes the supporting substances in the bones. Through exchange with –OH groups F enters the bone lattice structures as well as enamel and produces larger crystals more resistant to resorption. Fluoride thus accumulates in the body and absorbed F-ions bind Ca from food and blood. Formation of new bone is stimulated, resulting in the deformation and abnormal bone density (Ozha and Gilani, 2006). Fluoride also passes through the placenta and also appears in low concentration in saliva, sweat and lacteal secretion (milk).

Ingestion of F-ions decrease ionized calcium. This hypocalcaemia leads to changes in internal milieu of the body to maintain the Ca levels and leads to secondary hyperparathyriodism. The increased parathyroid hormone causes increased activity of osteoblasts in bone by activating membrane bound 3′5′ cycle AMP (Venkateshvarlu and Narayana, 1957).

This increased osteoblastic activity causes, increase in lactic acid released from ruffled border of osteoblasts. This causes increase in H^+ ion concentration, and hence lysis of lyposomes takes place. Release of lyposomal enzymes viz. acid protease, collagenase, hyaluronic acid in bones and other tissues of the body catalyses the reactions favoring the depolymerization of glycoprotein of bones and cartilages. This causes breakdown of hydroxy proline, which is responsible for stabilization of collagen triple helix. As the protein polymer desegregates and dissolves, the mineral binding capacity also get reduced and Ca is liberated, which helps in maintaining the serum Ca level. As a result the solubility of $Ca_5(OH)(PO_4)_3$ crystals also increases, causing its breakdown along with reduced laying down of collagen by decreasing hydroxylation of proline and lysine. This event simultaneously led to the elevation of the serum mucoprotein and polysaccharide levels. The net result of degradation of ground substance in bones and other calcified tissues like teeth leads to symptoms of fluorosis like delayed eruption of teeth, dental fluorosis and premature ageing (Gupta *et al.*, 1996).

7. Treatments and Prevention of Fluorosis

Fluorosis not only affects older persons, but there are ample evidences that even newborn baby and children of younger age have also been its victims. It not only affects the body of a person but also renders them socially, culturally and aesthetically crippled. There is a need to develop a well thought out strategy to attack this problem, which requires an urgent attention from both medical as well as of social workers. To summarize three approaches are suggested.

7.1 Health Education

Graphic presentation of the final consequences of the disease to the extent possible creates awareness about the disease. Live presentations of the patients who are suffering from the severe form of the disease in areas where the gravity of the problem has not reached to that extent help in implementing the need based preventive measures in the affected community.

7.2 Treatment of the Disease

Vitamin C and D, salts of Ca or Mg are prescribed in an attempt to reverse these effects. The presence of Ca in gut directly affects the absorption of F-ions and also improves serum levels. Vitamin D_3 in low doses enhances Ca absorption and retention without causing hypercalcaemia and thus directly affects the absorption of F-ions. It also inhibits the excessive release of parathyroid hormone there by checking excessive activation of osteoblasts thus preventing hyperosteoidosis and osteopenia. Vitamin C controls collagen formation, maintains the teeth structure and bone formation (Clerklewski, 1997).

7.3 Preventive Measures

7.3.1. Providing Defluoridated Water for Drinking Purpose: Methods of defluoridation recommended so far are aimed at bringing the F levels to the WHO standards. Desirable characteristics of defluoridation process, cost effectiveness, easy to handle, level of input F concentration, alkalinity, pH, T, no effect on taste of water, no addition of other undesirable substances (e.g. Al salts) to treat water are some parameters which are considered for adopting any of the defluoridation process. Some commonly used domestic defluoridation processes are :

7.3.1.1. Nalgonda Process: It looks a cumbersome process, not suitable for use by less educated population - the section that needs it the most. The process is used only for water having F content <10 ppm and turbidity <1500 ppm. There is a high residual Al content in output water. It is relevant to note that Al is a neurotoxin and concentration as low as 0.80 ppm of Al in potable water is reported to have caused Alzheimer's disease. The ISO 10500 for potable water sets an absolute level of 0.2ppm for Al that is well below the minimum value as reported in the output water, generated by this process. Also the taste of output water is generally not acceptable.

7.3.1.2 Activated Alumina Process: Reactivation of filter material is cumbersome and it is done only with the help of trained persons generally not available in most of our villages. This process also results in high residual Al in output water.

7.3.1.3. KRASS Process: This process differs from the known processes in its simplicity, cost effectiveness and only traces of residual Al in outlet water. There is no limit on F-concentration in input water. T, pH, alkalinity and TDS of input water do not affect this process. It is a practical approach especially for our rural population.

7.3.1.4 MTV Evaporator with Polymeric Heat Exchanger Process: This process works on mechanical vapor recompression principle with operating cost lower by 80% compare to conventional evaporators.

7.3.1.5 Other Processes: Electro-dialysis, ion exchange and reverse-osmosis are other processes that require special equipment, power, specially trained person to operate, need maintenance and are expensive. Keeping in view the cost involved in defluoridating the water it is desirable that the defluoridation of water should be restricted to potable water only.

7.3.2 Changing the Dietary Habits: (Nutritional Prophylaxis): Defluoridation of potable water alone does not bring the F level to safe limit. It would be necessary to overcome the toxic effects of the remaining F ingested through other sources. This is done by effecting minor changes in the diet and dietary habits of the population compatible with their social system and available resources. A properly designed nutritional regimen beneficially interferes with the toxic effects of fluoride. Vitamin C, Vitamin E and anti-oxidants, which are beneficial and are not very expensive, can be produced in rural areas without much investment.

- **Calcium:** Butter, Milk, Curd, Yoghurt, Jaggery, Drumstick, Sesame seeds , Sangari....
- **Vitamin C:** Aaonla, Karaunda, Lemon, Orange, Tomato, Sprouted cereals/pulses....
- **Vitamin E:** Vegetable oil, Nuts, Wheat grain cereals, Dried beans.....
- **Anti-oxidants:** Garlic, Ginger, Carrot, White onion, Papaya, Pumpkin and, Aloe vera, White mushroom, Pomegranate, Grap, Gogi Berries, Karaunda ......

All the above items have antagonistic effect; thereby play the prophylactic role in preventing fluorosis.

7.3.3 RWH (Alternative Water Source): Defluoridation of potable water for animals is costly and not feasible. Therefore the only solution of this problem is water harvesting. The water harvesting technology is aimed not only to provide F free water to human beings but also to animals.

8. Conclusions

All the above mentioned pronged attacks prove to be a blessing for the population especially for the younger generation living in F rich areas having no choice except to drink water contaminated with F and suffer inevitable consequences including permanent deformities. Fluoride affects the people and the animals as well. Therefore it is desirable that the animals should also be provided F free water for maintaining their longevity. Raising public awareness regarding fluorosis is critical. Beside, changing dietary habits, harvesting rainwater and promoting defluoridation of potable water at household level yield spectacular results in this regard. Various activities such as artificial recharge of groundwater, rejuvenation of traditional baoris-kunds, and judicious use of under groundwater for drinking and other purposes very well deal with the problem of fluorosis in the state. It is now desirable to test the various domestic defluoridation processes, especially in terms of acceptance by people without the need of any supervising agency and recommend suitable alternatives so that effective long-term implementation is achieved. Although F-intoxication through contaminated underground water is quite wide spread in Rajasthan, much of the tragedy can be prevented through proper education and development of groundwater resources in strata (aquifer), where Ca-concentration in groundwater is high. Educating the people and awakening civic responsibilities could make a major difference.

Withdrawal of the source(s) of fluoride entry to the body results in arrest of the progression of the disease and health complaints shall cease to exit. However, if speedy recovery is the aim, yet another intervention i.e. diet enriched by essential nutrients along with micro-minerals (Zn, Cu, Mg and Se) besides vitamins and other anti-oxidants need to be promoted through fruits and vegetables. An enriched diet ensures repair and maintenance of the damaged parts of the body, rise in haemoglobin and total recovery from the disease.

Water quality and health are interlinked. Therefore safe water is a matter of great concern in our country in general and Rajasthan in particular. Besides changing dietary habits, harvesting rainwater and promoting defluoridation of potable water at household level yield spectacular results in this regard. Authors suggest that remedial measures related to defluoridation technologies (viz. ion exchange, activated alumina and *reverse osmosis*) must be adopted in zones of excess F in groundwater to mitigate deleterious impact of F-toxicity on human health apart from artificial recharge of shallow aquifers.

REFERENCES

APHA, AWWA, and WPCF (1995) : "Standard Methods for Examination of Water and Waste Water, 19th Edition, NY, USA.

Chandra, S. (1983) : "Endemic Fluorosis in Rajasthan". *Indian Association of Preventive and Nutrition Research*, **17**, pp. 907-929.

Clerklewski, F.L. (1997) : "Fluoride Bio availability - Nutritional and Clinical Aspects".

Gupta, S.K., Gupta, R.C., Seth, A.K. and Gupta, A. (1996) : "A Reversal of Fluorosis in Children". *Acta Pediatrica Japonica*, **38**, pp. 513-19.

Maheshwari, R. (2004) : "The Fluoride Menace - A Review". *Agrobios News Letter*, **2**, III, pp. 11-13.

Maheshwari, R. (2006) : "Fluoride and Fluorosis in Rajasthan – Mitigating Fluoride Toxicity through Safe Drinking Water". *Proceedings of the International Conference and Expo on Botanical Products* (ICEBP-2006), Jaipur, India, March 219-229, 2006, pp. 37-53.

Maheshwari, R., Aroraa, C. and Singh, P. (2006)[c] : "Safe Water: Best Gift to the Futures Mankind". *Proceedings of State Seminar on Excess Fluoride in Potable Water and Its Associated Health Hazards (SEFPW-2006)*, Alwar, August 4 – 5, pp. 66-67.

Maheshwari, R. and Bansal, N. (2006) : "Excess Fluoride in Groundwater: Its Clinical Manifestations, Preventive Measures and Mitigation

Processes". *Proceedings of National Conference on Environmental Conservation (NCEC-2006)*, Pilani, September 1-3, pp. 130-120.

Maheshwari, R., Verma, S. and Pallavi (2006)[a] : "Fluoride Toxicity: An Alarming Environmental Threat". *Proceedings of International Conference on Toxicology, Toxicogenomics and Occupational Health (ICTTOH-2006) and 26th Annual Meeting of Toxicology (STOX)*, Gwalior, October 9-11, pp. 42.

Maheshwari, R., Yadav, R. N., Singh, P. and Karasawra, S. (2006)[b] : "Fluoride Toxicity: An Environmental Disaster". *Water Engineering News* **7**, V, pp. 7 – 9.

Mittal, A., Trivedi, N., Gupta, S.K., Kumar, S. and Gupta, R.K. (1993) : "Radiological Spectrum of Endemic Fluorosis: Relationship with Calcium Intake". *Skeletal Radiology*, **22**(4), pp. 257-61.

Ozha, D.D. and Gilani, F.M. (2006) : "Groundwater Levels, Consequent Health and Environmental Issues in Rajasthan – Integrated Management for Sustainable Future – Water for Life." *38th Annual convention, IWWA*-Jaipur, India, January 6-8, pp. 75-78.

Raani, B. (2004) : "Fluoride and Fluorosis in Rajasthan: An overview". *DNHE-A Project Report*, IGNOU, India.

Rock, W.P. and Sabiena, A.M. (1997) : "The Relationship between Reported Toothpaste Usage in Infancy and Fluorosis of Permanent Incisors". *British Dental Journal*, September 13, **183**(5), 165-70.

Susheela, A.K. (2006) : "The Present State of Knowledge on Fluoride and Arsenic in Drinking Water". *V Raman Endowment Lecture Manuscript, 38th Annual Convention IWWA*, Jaipur, January 6-8.

Venkateshwarlu, P. and Narayana, R.D. (1956) : *Indian Journal of Medicine Research*, **45**, pp. 377-385.

WHO (1996) : "Guidelines for Drinking Water Quality". *Health Criteria and other Supporting Information*, Geneva, **2**, III, Edition 2.

CHAPTER 15

Community Based Disaster Management

JAMES E. ROBERT

Director, Disaster Management Institute, Nairobi

Uganda Community Based Association for Child Welfare in Partnership with Huairou Commission and the Commission on Legal Empowerment for the Poor organized Grassroots Academy on Legal Empowerment on 17th November 2006 at Iganga District, Uganda.

Grassroots women from 17 districts participated in the academy and spent their time sharing and exchanging knowledge on legal empowerment for the poor and making recommendations for policy reform.

The participants highlighted the fact that as much as every Ugandan has a right to property and its protection as provided for by the constitution, many of the grassroots people are too poor to afford the acquisition of properties such as land.

It was also highlighted that those that have property like land, only have user rights. This situation is even worse in relation to rural and urban poor women and children.

Gender nd Social Issues

First Indian Management Congress Gender Session was viewed as a platform for debate using presentations that highlighted the role of women in response and rehabilitation especially after the tsunami and the floods in Western India. It was heartening to note the many examples of interventions from floods in Maharashtra, W.Bengal, Orissa and tsunami in Tamil

Nadu stressing the need to recognize the role of women as responders and actors in relief and rehabilitation.

Strengthening Community Trainers

Across the GROOTS International network there are grass-roots women's groups who have done innovative work to rebuild their communities after disasters or build resilient communities that can cope with disaster.

These innovators are disaster survivors themselves and are thus best equipped to train and teach other disaster hit communities on how they can shape resilience and recovery processes; and how they can change government, NGO and donor led programmes to the advantage of disaster affected families and communities.

As those who were present at the Grassroots Academy this summer know, the GROOTS International network in partnership with the American Jewish World Service is embarking on an innovative global initiative to build on the expertise of grassroots leaders in disaster prone areas to create a global network of grassroots women trainers who can be called upon to support and teach each other disaster affected communities. As part of this project, workshops bringing together grassroots leaders in three disaster-prone regions – Asia, Latin America and the Caribbean, and the 2004 tsunami affected region – were held in late November – early December 2006.

The Latin America and Caribbean Regional Workshop meeting was held from November 27 to December 1, 2006 in Kingston, Jamaica. It was hosted by the Construction Resource and Development Center, a grassroots women's organization that organized their community in response to Hurricane Ivan.

Twelve leaders from GROOTS member organizations Honduras, Jamaica and Peru came together to update each other on the strategies they are developing to teach through their disaster response teams. From communities struck yearly by hurricanes, tropical storms or small earthquake tremors, the three groups shared what strategies best represent their expertise.

Together, the women reflected on each other's strategies and the teaching tools they will make to transfer the strategies to other communities. At the end of the five days meeting, each group left with a plan to develop their teams over the next nine months.

Grassroots Academy, Uganda Strengthening Community Trainers: Jamaica, Latin America and Caribbean

Regional Workshop Report

Gender inequality can be subtle or explicit. It can mean more women die in disasters than men. Last year's *World Disasters Report* related how 3,972 women died when the Indian Ocean tsunami hit Ampara, Sri Lanka, compared with 2,124 men. In the Bangladesh cyclone of 1991, 71 women per 1,000 died compared with 15 men per 1,000 (aged 20–44). This has been blamed on male-to-male warning systems, women not getting men's permission to evacuate and cyclone shelters not designed for women's needs.

Women who survive disasters are often worse affected than men. According to American writer Kathleen Bergin, Hurricane Katrina was "a highly racialised and gendered event" which hit African-American women hardest. "More than half of the women in the city of New Orleans were single mothers, independently responsible for ensuring they and their children survived the storm," says Bergin.

Women's Community Role

Following all disasters, formal teams are set up in camps, villages and at higher administrative levels to manage disaster response.

But these often lack gender equity because:

• Socially constructed restrictions on mobility – especially regarding female safety –may prevent women from participating or restrictions for women to engage in activities outside the immediate family.

• Responsibility for multiple roles (e.g., domestic, childcare) leaves women little time for activities outside the home or workplace. Officials may lack gender awareness and see no need to engage women.

• Women themselves often lack confidence to play a public role – especially in male-dominated disaster management.

These barriers hinder women's participation in formal recovery–so specific measures are necessary to include women.

Windows of opportunity

Disasters, although destructive in so many ways, can open windows of opportunity for empowering women and enabling them to take an active role in building disaster-resilient communities.

In a world of unprecedented wealth, almost 2 million children die each year for want of a glass of clean water and adequate sanitation. Millions of women and young girls are forced to spend hours collecting and carrying water, restricting their opportunities and their choices.

The Human Development Report continues to frame debates on some of the most pressing challenges facing humanity.

On November 14-16, 2006 Swayam Shikshan Prayog and Groots International, supported by AJWS, organized the first of a series of workshops to strengthen community trainers on recovery and resilience.

The workshop brought young women leaders with a few months of experience face to face with senior leaders with more than ten years of experience. And the areas of expertise presented ranged from emergency response to organizing federations for enterprise and improving community access to health, water and sanitation.

After the tsunami and other disasters, Grassroots women's groups have done innovative work to rebuild their communities and are working to build resilient communities that can cope with future disaster. These innovators are disaster survivors themselves and are thus best equipped to train and teach other disaster hit communities on how they can shape resilience and recovery processes; and how they can change government, NGO and donor led programmes to the advantage of disaster affected families and communities.

ProVention Consortium, 2007

This ProVention project on Tools for Mainstreaming Disaster Risk Reduction supports this process, providing a series of 14 guidance notes for use by development organizations in adapting programming, project appraisal and evaluation tools to mainstream disaster risk reduction into development work in hazard-prone countries. The guidelines are deliberately intended as short, practical briefs supplementing existing more general guidelines on programming appraisal and evaluation tools.

Recovery to resilience: Strengthening community trainers

Human Development Report 2006—Beyond Scarcity: Power, Poverty and the Global Water Crisis

Tools for mainstreaming disaster risk reduction:

Guidance note for development organizations

For the Consultation Process with ISDR Stakeholders. 7 December 2006, the World Conference on Disaster Risk Reduction (WCDR, Kobe, Japan, 2005) represented a landmark in worldwide commitment to implementing a disaster reduction agenda. The 168 States attending the Conference adopted the Hyogo Framework for Action 2005-2015: Building the Resilience of Nations and Communities to Disasters (A/CONF. 206/6), which was endorsed by the General Assembly in resolution 60/195.

Developed through exhaustive negotiations between States, experts and collaborating organizations, the Framework's 10-year plan reflects the intention to take a holistic approach in identifying and putting into action complex multidisciplinary disaster risk reduction measures.

Strengthening the ISDR system: Background and Discussion Paper

High Level Commission on Legal Empowerment for the Poor (HLCLEP). One of the efforts to handle the poverty is by formulating a commission called Commission on Legal Empowerment for the Poor, which on 24-25 November, 2006 held a National Consultation in Jakarta. By looking the poverty condition and the efforts of Commission on Legal Empowerment for the Poor.

There are many creative ways—legal or extra legal—urban poor can conduct to comprehend their life cycle. These following are examples of their success.

River for our lives: In the early 2002, two kampongs at Surabaya's riverbanks namely, Nginden and Panjangjiwo have received letter of eviction from the local government. They continuously received second letter of eviction, and finally end up by eviction on houses in Nginden and Panjangjiwo located in the riverbank.

Statement of Action Grassroots Woman Network

The Center for Research on the Epidemiology of Disasters (CRED) releases today, 29 January 2007, the figures of disasters triggered by natural hazards for the year 2006. A total of 395 disasters were recorded in 2006 with 226 caused by floods, 66 by windstorms and 30 related to extreme temperature events. The 2006 disasters killed 21,342 people. While Asia was the continent hitted most by disasters triggered by natural hazards, three European countries - Netherlands, Belgium and Ukraine - ranked among the top ten countries most affected by deadly disasters. The economic damages in 2006 were around 19 billion US Dollars.

> 2006 Disasters in Numbers

> See the press release:

Centre for Research on the Epidemiology of Disasters December 2006

This issue is devoted to droughts and famines, which have devastated communities for centuries and continue to do so today. While droughts are relatively frequent phenomena, famines occur rarely. But when they do, the ferocity with which they affect populations does not compare with most other disasters.

Women and Children: The Double Dividend of Gender Equality.

The State of the World's Children 2007 reports on the lives of women around the world for a simple reason. Gender equality and the well-being of children go hand in hand. When women are empowered to live full and productive lives, children prosper. UNICEF's experience also shows the opposite. When women are denied equal opportunity within a society, children suffer. An assessment of capacities, gaps and opportunities towards building a comprehensive global early warning system for all natural hazards.

The present report synthesises the findings of this survey, which was carried out by the ISDR secretariat in collaboration with a multi-party working group established at the 11th session of the Inter-Agency Task Force on Disaster Reduction (IATF/DR) in May 2005.

Poor Success Stories

Disaster Data: A balanced perspective CRED Releases, the 2006 Disasters in Numbers

Global Survey of Early Warning Systems. UNISDR, The State of the World's Children 2007

Helena Molin Valdes, Deputy Director, ISDR Secretariat UN, Geneva.

Gender approach in disaster reduction is built on the understanding that both women and men are part of the same society, which as we know, does not mean we have the same rights, education and options to manage - nor in "normal" times, neither when a disaster strikes. Examples from recent tsunami-stricken South Asia, Central America, India and the Pacific, show that women can act as an agents of change. Several studies do confirm, however, that women are most of the time much worse affected than men when a disaster strike and less benefited when recovery begins. We therefore need to address the specific concerns of women already when designing disaster reduction policies and measures.

Women, disaster risk reduction and sustainable development: A gender perspective

Huairou Commission and GROOTS International are invited to participate in the upcoming two events in Nairobi, Kenya:

* Grassroots Academy: Building the Home-Based Care Alliance-June 30-July 2

* World YWCA's International Women's Summit: Women's Leadership Making a Difference on HIV and AIDS (July 4-7).

These events present an exciting opportunity to take account of grassroots women's efforts to provide care for the sick, support sustainable livelihoods, secure land tenure and property rights and engage with local authorities to increase transparency in aid distribution- all within the context of HIV and AIDS. The Academy will be a learning and teaching exchange between GROOTS Africa members and other members of the Huairou Commission and GROOTS International from Africa, Latin America, South Asia and the Asia Pacific. At the Summit, stakeholders ranging from YWCA delegates, women living with HIV and AIDS, researchers, activists, donors and representatives from governments, the United Nations and other multilateral agencies will attend.

CHAPTER 16

Disaster Management through Remote Sensing and GIS

VIKAS TAK

Department of Remote Sensing, MDS University, Ajmer

Introduction

It is well known fact that natural disasters strike countries, both developed and developing, causing enormous destruction and creating human suffering and producing negative impacts on national economics.

Due to diverse geo-climatic conditions prevalent in different part of the globe, different types of natural disaster like floods, droughts, earthquakes, cyclone, landslide, volcanoes, etc., strikes according to the vulnerability of the area.

India is considered as the world's most disaster prone country. It has witnessed devastating natural disaster in recent past like drought, flood, cyclones, earthquakes, landslides, etc.

Natural Disaster in India

India is a large country and prone to a number of natural hazards. Among all the natural disaster that country faces, river floods are the most frequent and often devastating. The shortfall in the rainfall cause droughts or drought like situation in various part of the country. The country has faced some severe earthquakes causing widespread damage to the life and property.

India has a coastline of about 8000 km which is prone to very severe cyclonic formation in the Arabian Sea and Bay of Bengal.

Another major problem faced by the country is in the form of landslide and avalanches.

Remote Sensing

Remote sensing makes observation of any object from a distance without coming into actual contact. Remote sensing can gather data much faster than ground based observation, and can cover large area at one time to give a synoptic view. Remote sensing comprises Aerial Remote Sensing which is the process of recording information, such as photographs and images from sensor on aircraft and Satellite. Remote Sensing which consists of several satellite remote sensing system which can be used to integrate natural hazard assessments into development planning studies. These are: Landsat, SPOT Satellite, Satellite Radar System, advanced very high resolution Radio. Satellite data is an indispensable tool for vulnerability assessment of human settlements and disaster management.

Geographic Information System, GIS

A GIS combines layers of information about a place to give you better understanding of place. What layers of information you combine depend on your purpose- finding the best location for a new store, analyzing environmental damage, viewing similar crimes in city to detect a pattern, and so on. Unlike with a paper map where "What you see is what you get"; a GIS map can combine many layer of information.

GIS provides a tool for effective and efficient storage and manipulation of remotely sensed data and other spatial and non-spatial data types for both scientific management and policy oriented information. This can be used to facilitate measurement, mapping, monitoring and modeling of variety of data types related to natural phenomenon.

The specific GIS application in the field of Risk Assessment are - Hazard mapping to show earthquake, landslides, flood or fire hazards. These map could be creator for cities, districts or even for the entire country and tropical cyclone. Threat maps are used by methodological departments to improve the quality of the tropical storm services and quickly communicate the risk to the people who are likely to get affected by the cyclone.

Manage disaster with GIS by using following steps –

- Assessing the location of risk and hazard in relation to population, property and natural resources.
- Integrating data and understanding the scope of an emergency to manage an incident.
- Recommending preventive and mitigating solutions.
- Determining how and where scarce resources should be assigned.
- Prioritizing for search and rescue tasks.
- Identifying staging area locations, operation of branches and divisions, and other important incident management needs.
- Assessing short or long-term recovery operation.

National Early Warning System for Tsunami and Storm Surges Background

Tsunami is a system of ocean gravity waves formed as a result of large-scale disturbance of the sea bed, mostly due to earthquakes (or volcanic eruptions or submarine landslides).

The Tsunami of December 26,2004-one of the strongest in the world which left over 250,000 dead and resulted in an estimated 43 billions dollars of damage.

Tsunamigenic Zones in Indian Ocean

For a tsunami to hit Indian coast, it is necessary that a tsunamigenic earthquake occurs and its magnitude should be larger than M7, and the possible locations of such events are enclosed in blue circle and ellipse.

The Imperatives and System Design

Tsunami detection - End - to - end

The Imperative - System Design

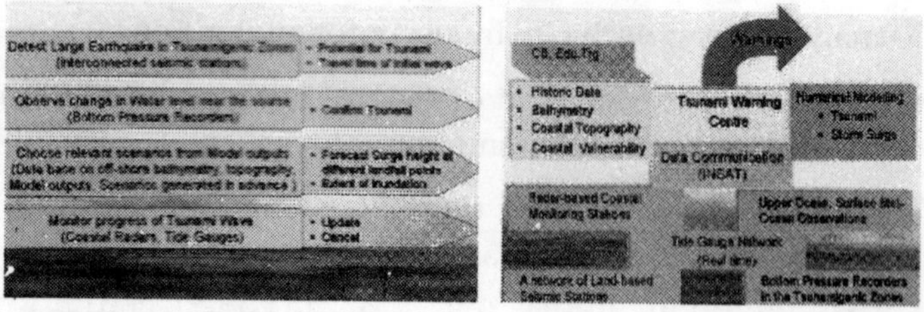

Observation Network

- Network of 17 broadband seismic stations for real-time Earthquake detection.
- Network of 12 Deep Ocean Assessment and Reporting Systems (DOARS) for detection of Tsunami Waves.
- Network of 50 Automatic tide gauges for monitoring the progress of Tsunami Waves.
- Other complimentary observations include 5 Coastal Radars, 2 Current Meter moorings, 26 Surface Drifters, 2XBT Lines and other Surface, Met-Ocean observing platforms.

Modeling

Use of numerical models to simulate all possible scenarios with varying earthquake source parameters.

Results indicating travel time and run-up heights at coastal locations will be organized in a database from which the closest scenario will be extracted at the time of event.

High-resolution bathymetry as well as coastal topography being generated for use in modeling. Detailed inundation maps will be generated for delineation of evacuation routes and long-term planning in vulnerable coastal communities.

Early Warning Centre

State-of-the-art Information and Communication Technology infrastructure for data reception, storage, modeling, display and alert systems, warning generation and dissemination.

Technical support facilities for 24X7 operations.

Decision support system and Standard Operating Procedure for warning generation and dissemination to designated contacts.

Partners

India is the only country that is developing capability to detect tsunami generated in the two tsunamigenic zones that would affect Indian Ocean.

India has been elected as Chairman of International Co-ordination Group (ICG) set up by UNESCO/IOC for Indian Ocean Tsunami Warning and Mitigation System, a network of 27 national systems.

India hosted the second session of ICG/IOTWS at Hyderabad during December 14-16, 2005.

International Interface

Institutions from Ministry of Earth Sciences (MoES), Department of Space (DOS), Department of Science and Technology (DST), Center for Scientific and Industrial Research (CSIR), Ministry of Home Affairs (MHA), Ministry of External Affairs (MEA).

CHAPTER 17

Disaster Management - An Integrated Effort

RAVINDER KUMAR

Lecturer of Geography, Govt. Lohia PG College, Churu (Rajasthan)

Introduction

Disaster means a catastrophic mishappening, calamity of grave occurrence in any area, arising from natural or man-made causes, or by accident or negligence. Disasters are events that cause widespread damage, destruction and human sufferings. It requires immediate, coordinated and effective response by govt., community, volunteers and corporate sector organisations.

Impact of Disaster

Disaster leads to

- Loss of life, property, livelihood, health and quality of life.
- Deceleration in the economy.
- Depreciation in Domestic currency.
- Greater indebtedness.
- Major setbacks to economic development and social development.
- Setback to community development efforts.

Elements of Reforms

- Introduction of a well coordinated comprehensive approach in Disaster Management.
- Adaptation of an internationally best practice risk reduction model.
- Creation of an enabling environment for the implementation of the national risk reduction initiative.
- Development of strategic policy and programming framework.

National Platform for Risk Reduction

Five strategic areas

- Professionalising the Disaster Management System.
- Mainstreaming and Partnerships.
- Community empowerment.
- Expanding risk reduction across a broader range of hazards.
- Strengthening response system.

Prevention, Mitigation and Preparedness

Disaster Prevention	*Disaster Mitigation*	*Disaster Preparedness*
Activities designed to provide permanent protection from disaster.	Measures taken in advance of a disaster aimed at reducing its impact on society and the environment.	Ability to predict, respond to and cope with the effect of a disaster.

Disaster Management Continuum

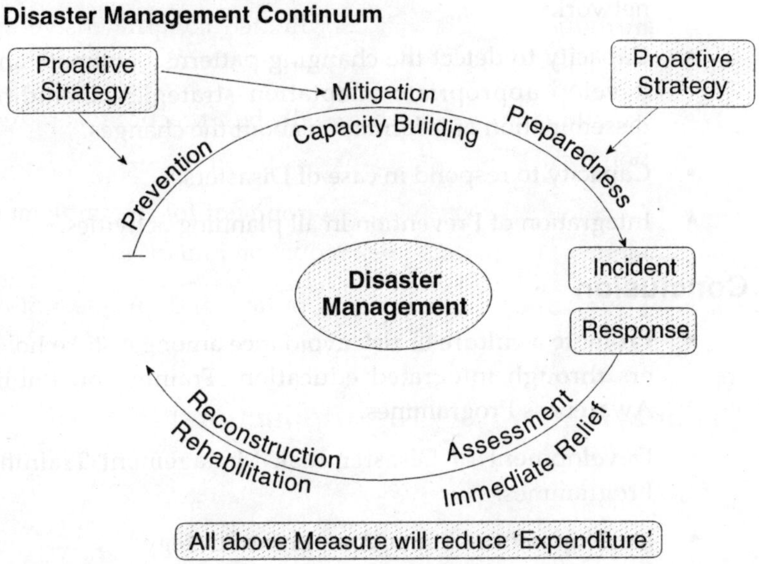

Strengths of the Corporate Sector

There was great role played by corporate sector in recent Disasters like Gujarat Earthquake, Orissa Super Cyclone, Tsunami, Mumbai Flood and Surat Flood. In addition to financial responsibility, corporate sector can contribute significantly to :

- Introduction of new Ideas, Technology, Innovative approach, Management Skills.
- Equipments/resource inventory.
- Risk transfer mechanism (Insurance Products).
- Flexibility and Speed of implementation.

Challenges

- Capacity to provide timely and accurate warning upto the community level.

- Capacity to maintain and operate adequate operation networks.
- Capacity to detect the changing patterns of climate and develop appropriate adaptation strategies, including dissemination of information about the changes.
- Capacity to respond in case of Disasters.
- Integration of Prevention in all planning activities.

Conclusion

- Promote a culture of risk avoidance amongst stake holders through integrated education, Training on Public Awareness Programmes.
- Development of Disaster Risk Management Training Programmes.
- Development of Public Awareness Strategy.
- Promotion of risk avoidance behaviour.
- Focusing on research programmes.